# NINE CLINICAL CASES:

## The Soul of Pastoral Care and Counseling

Raymond J. Lawrence

Cover photo by Lauren Kuo.

# Dedication

This book is dedicated to my four delightful and idiosyncratic children: Christopher Moore Lawrence, Chrysanthi Lawrence, Anastasia Lawrence, and Lauren Kay-Jin Kuo.

# Table of Contents

Dedication ................................................................5

Table of Contents ........................................................6

Preface ..................................................................8

Acknowledgements .........................................................10

Foreword
by Robert Charles Powell, M.D., Ph.D. ....................................11

CASE 1
LeeAnn, a 12-year-old Girl
With Cystic Fibrosis......................................................13

CASE 2
Erica, the Mother of a Two-year-old
With Cancer...............................................................19

CASE 3
A 17-year-old Girl Paralyzed .............................................25

CASE 4
A Nigerian Immigrant in Britain Under
the Spell of Witches......................................................32

CASE 5
A Feisty British Woman Veteran Is
Ready To Die..............................................................39

CASE 6
A Young Man Conflicted Over
Sexual Identity...........................................................44

CASE 7
A Canadian Veteran at the
End of His Life ..........................................................53

CASE 8
David, a Mature Man Dying of
Pancreatic Cancer.........................................................60

CASE 9
A Native American Family Attends to
the Dying of Their Matriarch ....................................................................65

REFLECTIONS ON
DAVID B. MCCURDY'S
Ethical Issues in Case Study Publication ...............................................70

GENERAL CRITICISM OF THE BOOK
*Spiritual Care in Practice:*
*Case Studies in Healthcare Chaplaincy* .................................................76

EPILOGUE: THE SPIRITUAL PROBLEM ................................................81

ABOUT THE AUTHOR ...........................................................................88

# Preface

This work is indebted first to George Fitchett and Steve Nolan who published their work, *Spiritual Care in Practice: Case Studies in Healthcare Chaplaincy* (published by Jessica Kingsley Publishers of London and Philadelphia) earlier this year. Their work is the foundation on which this book is written. While their work has flaws, and what work doesn't, they have forged new ground in offering up a volume of specific clinical pastoral cases followed by critical comment. In other words, they have put into one volume nine pastoral care cases followed by critical comment. They have thus put in writing the essence of the clinical pastoral training process begun almost a century ago by Anton T. Boisen. For this they are to be commended.

This book is actually little more than an expanded book review of the Fitchett-Nolan book. For each of the nine cases and for each of the three associated critiques, I have provided a summary. Following that, I add my own critique of each case itself and of each associated critique. Following that is a summary and critique of the chapter on ethical concerns by David B. McCurdy. Finally, I set the entire book in the context of the clinical pastoral training tradition.

Most of the published work on clinical pastoral supervision seems to have focused on principles and theory. The value of the Fitchett-Nolan work is that it is based on specific clinical cases, the nine cases that are published in the book itself. I hope they will have set the standard for future publications. Theory is useful, but nothing is quite as useful nor quite as engrossing as a specific clinical case.

Fitchett, in his introduction to the book, argues for more published cases in the clinical pastoral training field. The current paucity of published clinical cases is actually puzzling in that the movement itself began a century ago with the study of cases. The founder of clinical pastoral training, Anton Boisen, actually made himself and his personal troubles the principal "case." Therefore, I second Fitchett's call for more published cases in the field as the best route for learning the art and science of pastoral care, counseling and psychotherapy.

The work that follows is a running commentary on the 9 cases as well as the 27 commentaries on the cases and on the summary essay, *"Ethical Issues in Case Study Publication."* In addition to the two editors, six additional persons appear as critics of some of the cases. For better or for worse, I have commented on each and every one.

I have elected throughout not to name the specific chaplains whose work is included herein. I am not thereby keeping a confidence. Their names and current positions are clearly identified in the Fitchett-Nolan book itself. But I am electing not to expose them further. I prefer to grant them what meager privacy yet available to them, which is not much.

I actually feel some admiration for the nine who put their clinical pastoral work on view for all the world to see—and to pick apart. It is a very courageous choice to put one's work in the public arena for scrutiny. It is also potentially hurtful, particularly if one has thin skin, and, more so, if one has enemies eager to enter the fray for purposes of devaluation. No one is without flaws. No professional works without missteps. And no one is immune to certain blindnesses. But few would choose to lay their flaws and missteps open to public scrutiny. We have to applaud the courage of these presenting chaplains and pastoral counselors who have laid their professional work open to public examination in this book. They have my admiration and my esteem.

But, as the reader will see, I have not elected to coddle or to consider the feelings of the presenters of the nine cases published here. I am assuming that they are professionals prepared to receive straightforward critique of their work. Nor do I spare their published critics. Nor do I myself expect to be spared strong rebuttal, particularly in instances where I might have been wrong or uninformed.

Let the conversation begin.

# Acknowledgements

I want to express my appreciation to David Roth for first encouraging me to write this book. I want to thank Perry N. Miller for his weighty encouragement to write in general, and specifically on this subject, and for reviewing this text, making a number of proposed revisions, and finally for publishing parts of the first draft in *Pastoral Report* (cpsp.org), the newsletter of the College of Pastoral Supervision and Psychotherapy. I also want to express my deep appreciation to Cynthia Olson who expertly proofed every page, and who is a copy editor extraordinaire! If any malaprops or typos exist, they belong to me in making last-minute changes and additions. Finally, my thanks to Howard Pendley and John Sabean, who also reviewed the text and made a number of common-sense suggestions that proved to be quite felicitous. And finally, I want to thank Krista Argiropolis for her expertise in moving the text from cyberspace to a physical object, an actual book.

# Foreword

## by Robert Charles Powell, M.D., Ph.D.

This book starts off as an extended critique of Fitchett and Nolan's *Spiritual Care in Practice*. It ends up as a detailed reminder of how Anton Boisen's clinical histories—in contrast to those in the book Lawrence reviews—focused more on the patients than on the practitioners. "Ends up," indeed! Lawrence's trenchant epilogue by itself is worth the price of the book. That being said, I recommend reading the whole thing, and here's why:

In this day and age of "spiritual assessment tools," perhaps we could use reminding that the Boisenesque tradition is not against gathering data. The goal, however, has a distinctive focus, not on the needs of the institution—to check certain boxes, to dot certain i's and cross certain t's—but on the specific, idiosyncratic needs of those who are suffering, bewildered, or vulnerable. Boisen strove for "genuine interest in the patient and his [or her] problems"—for "discovery and solving of the patient's actual difficulties" [*The Exploration of the Inner World* (1936), p.245]. The patient's problems and difficulties might not fit into some predetermined schema.

Likewise, in this day and age of diagnosis-specific "techniques," perhaps we could use reminding that the Boisenesque tradition is not against heuristic theory. The interest, however, is more in the patients' theories and techniques with regard to their unique situations than in societies' constructs *du jour*. Maybe a patient views his or her dilemmas primarily through feminist, racist, economic, or ethnic "glasses"—but maybe not. As Lawrence counsels, "The proper posture of a clinical chaplain is agnostic, regardless of the chaplain's own personal beliefs and allegiances. The clinical role demands it." If we try to engage patients within enough time and space, perhaps they will find within us—consciously or unconsciously—bits of the empathic caring they need.

Now, some 90 years after Boisen created the field of clinical pastoral practice, perhaps chaplaincy could use more theological sensitivity, more clinical seriousness, more sincere curiosity, and, above all, more attentive listening—with "a third ear," so to speak, for patients' conscious, preconscious, and unconscious meaningful connections. Lawrence, through his critique, reminds us that Boisenesque clinical pastoral chaplaincy calls for understanding rather than proselytizing of the patient, however well meant that proselytizing of social or religious creed might be.

As usual, Lawrence is polite, but doesn't mince words. He says a lot of things that have needed to be said for quite some time. Among other things, he offers a coherent analysis of why the notion of "spiritual care" is not equivalent to, or an adequate substitute for, the notion of "pastoral care." It could be very, very interesting if a set of editors could take to heart Lawrence's commentaires and assemble an even better collection of case histories in clinical pastoral chaplaincy. So, go ahead and write a thoughtful rebuttal to Lawrence's critique! As he says in his preface, "Let the conversation begin!"

# CASE 1
# LeeAnn, a 12-year-old Girl
# With Cystic Fibrosis

## I. The Case

The patient is a 12-year-old girl stricken with a daunting disease, cystic fibrosis. Her options are limited. Her life likely will be short and confined, under conditions of rather extreme isolation from peers and loved ones. Her family's home is a long distance away from the hospital, and she is alone most of the day. She has had more than a hundred surgeries in her short life. The chaplain, who has committed only a quarter of his time to clinical work, and the rest to research, generously notes at least ten substantive visits with her over the course of a year, visits that included burdensome infection-control measures such as gowns, face masks, and gloves. In short, the patient presents a heartrending case that is almost unbearable to read.

Though the chaplain was acquainted with the patient and her mother from previous visits to the outpatient clinic, the first of what the chaplain calls a significant pastoral visit occurs while the patient is an inpatient. The chaplain's intention is to build a relationship with the patient and to assess what follow-up might be warranted. The conversation was wide-ranging. Noting a book on ghosts on the bedside table, the chaplain initiates a conversation about ghosts, and then angels, and finally asks whether the patient ever talks to God. The patient admits to having an active prayer life and says her prayers are mostly about other people and about her cystic fibrosis. The chaplain then asks if God could come here what two questions would she ask, or what two things would she want God to say to her. According to the chaplain, she was "intrigued," but "at a loss for an answer." The chaplain suggests she think about the question as homework, to which she readily agreed. The chaplain assessed this as a successful beginning, in that LeeAnn evidenced significant spiritual resources, e.g., a belief in God, a positive image of God, and an active prayer life.

The second pastoral visit three days later found LeeAnn alone again. While setting up a board game, LeeAnn remarked on the earlier question of what she would ask God, and she decided the question would be, "What do you want me to do?" The chaplain responds, "And how do you think God would answer?" "Help others?" LeeAnn asks. God would be pleased with your answer, the chaplain assures her.

The third pastoral visit began with a board game. Between turns the chaplain asks how she keeps from being bored. Her grandparents are coming that night, and she plays board games with nurses and staff, and she likes to draw. The chaplain then asks if she still feels like God was with her, or if she talked with God. No response is indicated. The chaplain then offers two invitations: one, that they pray together, and two, that LeeAnn agree to be part of a case study. The patient readily agreed to both offers. The chaplain assesses a deepened pastoral relationship, indicated by the fact that LeeAnn brightened and put aside her computer when the chaplain appeared.

In the fourth visit, the chaplain wonders out loud whether LeeAnn might "draw a picture of herself sick, and of God." LeeAnn produces a quite primitive drawing of God and some stick figures. The chaplain offers a prayer, making reference to the drawing. The chaplain documents in the chart that LeeAnn is ready for discharge because "she had discussed and practiced spiritual religious practices as a coping mechanism through prayer and drawing."

On the fifth visit, the following day, the chaplain referred back to the drawing and inquired what LeeAnn thought about God and cystic fibrosis when she wasn't sick. She declared that God was telling the doctors the right medicine to give her, and the chaplain concludes that he has hit pay dirt. The chaplain was then forced to depart by another clinician who took precedence and required time with the patient.

The sixth encounter occurred in the waiting room of the cystic fibrosis clinic. This was the first chance for the chaplain to discuss with LeeAnn's mother his proposal for writing up a case study on LeeAnn. The public nature of the waiting room inhibited conversation. Nevertheless, the chaplain asked LeeAnn, "how she and God were doing," and if she and her mother would like prayer. They assented. Their positive affect, according to the chaplain, showed that they valued the prayer.

The seventh encounter came five months later when LeeAnn was admitted for a bacterial infection in her lungs. LeeAnn has a computer with her but no drawing material. She asks the chaplain if he can provide her with drawing materials. He offers no prayer this time.

On the eighth visit, the next day, the chaplain brought in drawing material and asks LeeAnn if she would be interested in drawing as a different way of praying. And of course she would.

Two days later the chaplain brings more drawing material, reminding her that this was more material for her to engage in drawing and praying. She takes out her markers and goes to work.

In the tenth and last substantive visit, the chaplain again raised the subject of drawing and praying, and he concludes that LeeAnn has accepted this new way of praying.

Subsequent visits in the clinic are less frequent and are not described. LeeAnn is admitted again and more talk about drawing and praying ensues.

In his summary the chaplain makes a strong argument that he functions out of a narrative theory, and he cites Arthur Frank as a strong proponent for allowing the story to be told the way the narrator needs to tell it. He believes he succeeded in that role. He also believes that LeeAnn held to a positive image of God and felt well connected to God and her family. He also believes he allowed LeeAnn to tell her story the way she chose to tell it. And he concludes that cystic fibrosis is caused by genetic mutations, rather than by God.

## II. The Published Critiques

The co-editor critic (Steve Nolan) essentially recapitulates the chaplain's role in eliciting what he calls LeeAnn's restitution narrative, although the presented clinical data does not support such a claim. He does add that the requirement for donning the paper gown, facemask, and gloves during visits must have been a very troublesome burden both to patient and chaplain. The critique is quite positive otherwise.

The chaplain critic (Alister W. Bull) states that the chaplain seemed to have a settled viewpoint, and that this case did not change his perspective but rather confirmed that his approach was appropriate. He adds that healthcare chaplaincy has not reached a point where there is an agreed upon approach to assessment of cases. He offers this "more as an observation than a criticism," but indicates this lack of clarity may weaken the distinctive contribution that chaplaincy can bring. The critic's sharpest criticism is that the chaplain's affirmation of the patient's view of God and guiding the patient toward prayer could indicate a subconscious power play on the chaplain's part. But he adds that this is not to suggest any abuse of power on the part of the chaplain. Then he comes back later to write that he "felt ambiguous [sic] about the religious focus that emerged in this case [and in the other two pediatric cases], as many assumptions about belief about God are left unaddressed."

The psychologist critic (Sian Cotton) assumes that the chaplain's regular visits to LeeAnn were a source of positive strength to her, but notes that he did not report asking about her emotional functioning. He wonders if the chaplain's relationship-building with LeeAnn is an end unto itself, or a path toward clinical, professional, and spiritual outcomes. But he does not think there is a right answer to this. He suggests it might have been useful to inquire of LeeAnn about what it was like for her to have so many hospitalizations and disconnections from friends.

## III. The Author's Perspective

I am not convinced that we heard the authentic voice of LeeAnn in this case. The voice I hear is that of a compliant child in relation to an authoritative adult. Hoping for a 12-year-old to feel free enough to talk candidly with an adult, even after a 5-year relationship, may be more than can be wished for. Thus, the chaplain's apparent failure to hear the authentic voice of the patient may have been predestined. To be sure, the chaplain's perpetual beating of the drum for prayer and God voided any hope of the patient's sharing anything significant about her own grim experience. She undoubtedly feels harassed by a propagandist for God.

The nadir of the chaplain's inappropriateness came on a visit to the outpatient clinic where he found mother and daughter together for the first time. He asked the girl "how she and God were doing." Such a question to a preadolescent could be considered crazy-making, as well as inappropriately evangelistic. Even mature adult human beings who are sane will never know with any clarity how they are doing with God—if indeed there is a God. How could they? For an adult authority figure to ask a child a question that cannot be answered is sadistic.

As suggested by the psychologist critic, Cotton, it would have been sufficient for the chaplain to have asked simply, "What's it like for you here in isolation?" or, "What's it like for you being so far from home in a strange place?" or, "What's it like for you to have to be protected by all this gear and equipment?" or, "How much do you miss your family?" She may or may not have ever been able to respond freely and talk about herself in that way with an adult stranger in the form of a chaplain. We can be sure she would have understood the questions; however, the question, "How are you doing with God?" is not a question she would have any way to answer. Even the chaplain, if he were honest, would be flummoxed by such a question put to him. The question itself is crazy-making, and directed by an adult to a child is predatory.

I suggest here that the failure of this chaplain to ask questions that might have evoked the girl's pain and sorrow and despair can be explained by the chaplain's avoidance of pain in his own life. That would mean, in Boisen's terms, that his own counter-transference inhibited his ability to touch the girl's pain. He preferred to take the role of religious functionary, defending himself against the profound pain he likely would feel in identifying with her should she disclose herself to him. Boisen's clinical training movement was designed to engage pastors with their own unconscious and transferential material, which in turn might sensitize them and make them aware enough to hear the pain of others. This chaplain would likely benefit from further clinical training, where with a competent supervisor he might understand what is buried in him that leads him to look away from the terrible pain of this 12-year-old. And worse it is to cover it up with God-talk.

To give him due credit, the chaplain who has known the patient over a five-year period, generously spends significant time sitting with the young patient playing board games and drawing. These activities might have led to some opening in the patient whereby she might have been empowered to share some of her painful experience, which to any observer would appear unspeakably grim. But the chaplain can't wait for the patient to start feeling free to talk. He wants her to pray and to talk to God, and without delay. In nine of the ten noted visits the chaplain lobbies for the girl to talk with God and to pray.

The chaplain in question turns the Boisen model on its head. Instead of seeking to hear the voice of the young girl in a desperate plight, he moves to instruct her in the practices of Christian piety. He is hell-bent on persuading her to pray. He's as heavy-handed as an evangelist at a tent revival calling for a belief in Jesus.

# CASE 2
# Erica, the Mother of a Two-year-old With Cancer

## I. The Case

Erica is the mother of a two-year-old girl with cancer, admitted to the emergency room. There are several young children at home, a grown daughter, and a new husband who doesn't understand Erica's religious affections. She describes herself as a "redneck" with a faith in Jesus that was making it possible for her to cope. God has spoken to her directly and powerfully, and she relates stories about the voices. Erica is certain that God has a plan, but she is not sure why God would speak to her. She keeps all this from her husband, who "couldn't understand. "

Erica had requested a chaplain when admitted to the ER. She responded negatively to the first chaplain she met, a female who was "dressed too fancy," unlike the present chaplain who is dressed down, in blue jeans and turtleneck. The chaplain responds to Erica's sharing of her experience of God speaking to her by relating the story of God talking to Moses.

Later Erica rants over the many misleading translations of the Bible in current circulation, arguing that only the King James Version is authentic. She is vexed specifically that the new translations do not declare Mary a "virgin." In response the chaplain offers a mini-lecture on the problems of translating ancient manuscripts. It did not seem to occur to the chaplain that Erica may have some thoughts or feelings about virginity itself, or perhaps the circumstances of her own deflowering, and thus might have become fixed on this biblical text.

It appears that every chaplain visit is ended with a prayer, and sometimes at the chaplain's own request.

The chaplain reports an intuition along the way that Erica might have a substance abuse problem that she was not disclosing. This would seem to be a good guess. In response to this supposition, the chaplain decides to divulge her own past history of substance abuse. She took this action, she says, subsequent to a message from the social work department reporting that Erica had made a request there for referral to a "Christian counselor" for help with one of her older children. The chaplain discloses her knowledge of this request by advising Erica to find a *competent* counselor rather than a specifically Christian one. There is no inquiry and no speculation as to why Erica went to social workers for referral and not to the chaplain herself. One would think this would have been an insult and a negative reflection on the pastoral relationship itself, a devaluation of the chaplain's authority and/or wisdom. Yet, that is not explored.

Erica and the chaplain appear to have some difficulty finding places to talk in private. Or perhaps Erica's need to smoke is the motivation to exit the hospital. In any case, the two of them devise a plan to move outside to a nearby street corner and to sit on the curb while they talk and Erica smokes. It is in that context that the chaplain shares her own substance-abuse history and her 12-step program experience. This is a rather poignant picture, an institutional chaplain counseling on the street, sitting on the curb. If nothing else, this chaplain is resilient.

At one point Erica's husband arrived unexpectedly in the hospital room while the chaplain was present. Erica suddenly fired four shots with a toy gun that emits plastic globs, leaving him nonplussed. Erica immediately proposed to go for a private conversation with the chaplain, leaving the husband with their daughter.

The chaplain reports that every visit with Erica began and ended with a hug, and it seems to have been a serious hug at least some of the time. One such incident is described as Erica holding her baby and sobbing, throwing herself into the chaplain's arms, while the chaplain embraced them both and stroked Erica's back as she prayed.

In her summary, the chaplain assesses herself in relation to this patient as eager to get religion out of the way so that spiritual care could begin, and to move the conversation to a deeper level.

She feels she became Erica's "mentor and spiritual friend."

The chaplain also contends that she has been "a transitional object" for Erica, as described by the psychoanalytic authority, D.W. Winnicott. Very few readers will have any idea what a transitional object means, or whether it promotes understanding of the pastoral role here.

# II.  The Published Critiques

The co-editor's (Steve Nolan) assessment of the case is that Erica had "a keen Christian faith," that the chaplain "models good practice in multi-professional working," and that she models "an incarnational approach." The editor also notes that while self-disclosure can be a first step towards "violating the boundaries of the therapeutic relationship," the chaplain here "offers chaplains an example of good practice in this sensitive area."

The other two critical assessments are more substantive—and more accurate. The clinical chaplain critic (Alister W. Bull) seems to be mostly undecided and feeling ambivalent about this case, but he does question the chaplain's identification of herself as a Winnicotian "transitional object." He also "felt ambiguous" about the religious focus that emerged in the case. Even more telling, he felt that the chaplain "may have had her own deconstructive agenda" in her claim that her goal was "to get religion out of the way" in favor of spirituality. He also "wonders," astutely, about the chaplain's compliance with Erica's request to leave her child and husband in the room (after shooting him!) while the two of them went off to talk.

The psychologist critic (Sian Cotton) is somewhat more decisive and direct. He says the researcher in him wants to know what is the definition of "spiritual care", and if the chaplain is off-loading religion in its favor. He certainly belled the cat on that one. I suggest he better not wait around for an answer.

# III. The Author's Perspective

We have here a very complex and troublesome clinical case, followed by three critical responses. It should be said first that the chaplain deserves credit for courageously jumping into water over her head, publicly disclosing a number of poignant and serious issues, and making herself the object of public scrutiny. She certainly should get high marks for courage. Maybe we can all learn from her commitment as well as her mistakes.

I strongly second the psychologist critic (Cotton) who asks for a definition of spiritual care that is distinct from religious or pastoral care. As I have already suggested, I believe that will be hard to come by. No one should look for it anytime soon.

As for the other clinical responses, I concur with the chaplain critic (Bull), but with less ambivalence. Contrariwise, I take issue with the co-editor's (Nolan) assessment of Erica's "keen Christian faith," and that the chaplain is a model of an incarnational faith. For the latter point, I do not know what he is talking about. The chaplain is certainly *in the flesh,* probably too much so, if that is what is meant by an incarnational stance. As for Erica's faith, it seems to me a borderline or even psychotic construct. Persons today often refer to God speaking to them, typically meaning, "metaphorically speaking." But Erica sounds as if she is not speaking in metaphors. She suggests that she may in fact be hearing voices, in which case she would seem to qualify as psychotic, or at least borderline.

Now, there is nothing wrong with being psychotic, or borderline. Anton Boisen taught us that lesson well. But the question is how to work with a person in such straits. The best answer yet is that we should listen to them, and keep listening until we can make some sense out of their irrational thought processes. My problem with Erica's chaplain is that she does not seem to recognize that she may have an exceedingly troubled woman on her hands. And the chaplain does not do much listening. She lectures on the Bible and engages in discussion of the meaning of the Trinity. She shares her own past history of substance abuse. She prays and prays *ad nauseum.* She hugs.

But she does not really listen in depth. She does not seem to wonder what might underlie Erica's troubling personal disorganization.

For example, what might it mean that Erica shoots her husband with the toy gun in the presence of the chaplain, and then whisks the chaplain away from her husband for a private talk? Shouldn't it be useful for the chaplain and for Erica to meet and converse jointly with the husband? Is the chaplain no more than Erica's pawn in this family drama?

I am also concerned about the extraordinary amount of physical contact that takes place between the chaplain and Erica, an issue only lightly touched upon by one of the critics, the clinical chaplain (Bull). The boundary between the two seems much too permeable. Hugs at the beginning and end of each visit, along with intimate back-rubs during prayers while Erica sobs. A male chaplain acting in such a way would place himself in grave danger in the current environment of sexual hysteria. But political issues aside, most authorities in the field consider such physical intimacy to be inhibitory to a significant pastoral or counseling relationship. I doubt that the permeable physical boundaries between Erica and the chaplain are useful in furthering the therapeutic process.

I also wonder about the wisdom of the chaplain's self-disclosure of her own history of substance abuse. As with the issue of physical contact, this seems to be the consequence of boundaries that are too permeable.

In spite of all I have written, I am quite struck by the articulate, if somewhat skewed, closing words of the chaplain writing in her own self-defense for this case: "So I believe that the most important part of the work I will ever do is *inner* work, plumbing my own fears and chaos so that I will not pull away from the fears and chaos of others."

Agreed. Well said. She is eminently correct, as far as she goes. And the chaplain in this case, indeed, did not pull away from Erica's chaos.

But it's like a reverse of the old parable of falling over backwards while trying to avoid falling on one's face. It could be said that the chaplain fell on her face, but did avoid falling over backwards.

The chaplain blessedly did not pull away from Erica's chaos, but she did get swallowed up in it, and thus lost her way and abandoned her role. The chaplain must revise her philosophy of pastoral care, and resolve neither to pull away *nor to get swallowed up,* but to remain close and intimate, while remaining distinct and separate, and watching with a third eye...and patiently listening until some sense of meaning in the craziness begins to emerge from the patient herself. It often takes a long time.

This case is an excellent teaching instrument from which we all can learn. I do hope the chaplain can endure the critique in the service of her own learning as well.

# CASE 3
# A 17-year-old Girl Paralyzed

## I. The Patient

Angela is a blonde, blue-eyed, petite 17-year-old who, after a family argument, lost control of her car on an icy road and suffered a severed upper spine. She was paralyzed from the neck down, with no prospect of remedial treatment, suddenly an almost certain lifelong quadriplegic.

The female Catholic chaplain visited her for four "rapport-building visits" and then used the Spiritual Assessment Tool designed by the spirituality guru, Christina Puchalski, who also wrote the forward to the book. The Spiritual Assessment Tool recommends putting the following questions to the patient:

- Do you have spiritual or religious beliefs that help you cope during this time?

- What importance do your beliefs have for you at this time?

- Are you a member of a religious or spiritual community?

- Are there any particular spiritual or religious activities important to your well-being while you are in the hospital?

On reading this list of four, my first thought was that if I were a patient suffering from such a catastrophic, life-altering event, and a chaplain came asking me such questions, I would call security and have them removed from my room. My second fantasy was that if in the unlikely event I had any spirit left in me I might play with the chaplain and reply to the first question, "Yes. My god is a large cosmic cat who is coming soon to deliver me from this nightmare and take me to cat heaven."

The basic theology of Puchalski is that religion is something like a Swiss Army Knife, a little tool with many uses that often comes in handy in a pinch. That's what you get when you turn a physician into an expert on pastoral care and counseling.

Next, the chaplain used what she calls her own specially devised "Spiritual Assessment Tool" that leads to discussions of how patients feel centered or anchored, called or motivated, whether they feel connected to relationships beyond themselves, and contribute to the good of the world and/or the good of others in grand or small ways. It is not clear why the chaplain needed two sets of so-called Spiritual Assessment Tools. One seems about as inhumane as the other. The chaplain wrote that she weaves the questions into conversations, presumably in order that the patient will not feel surveyed.

Angela, it turned out, was a member of a small Protestant church but had not been attending or engaging in any religious practices. Yet she was now praying several times a day and having the Bible read to her. Obviously she could not lift the book to read on her own.

For the first few days after her accident, Angela was in denial, expecting to go home soon. Her mother, too, was in denial, promising her that if Angela prayed hard enough, God would give her a miracle. And, of course, the chaplain was asked by Angela to pray for that same miracle, which she did. (What are chaplains for anyway?)

The chaplain thought Angela to be coping adequately in the early days after the accident, though she thought Angela to be unaware of the likely permanence of the injury. But it would have been clear to any clinical observer that Angela was in massive denial. During this period, the chaplain discussed with Angela how God was working in her life. The chaplain believed that God is always with us, especially in our deepest darkness. That Angela has just been made a quadriplegic, but that God is with her, is the ultimate *non sequitur* driven by denial.

Angela's pastor came to visit, but the chaplain reported that Angela does not relate to him.

Into the second week of hospitalization, Angela's illusions, hopes, and prayers began to fade. She stopped caring for herself, refused to work with the psychologist, and stopped eating and drinking. Nevertheless, the chaplain persevered in her visits, laying aside her "spiritual resources" agenda and most of her pious defense of God, and finally began to listen quietly to Angela's despair. "I have lost everything! Absolutely everything!" was her cry. And so it seems. Who in the world would not feel exactly the same way? The chaplain finds the emotional barrage a bit disorienting and difficult to bear, but she is for a space of time blessedly quiet, finally. The chaplain silently comforts herself (but not Angela, thank God!) with the belief that God is with us always, even in our deepest darkness. And it appears that the chaplain blessedly and to her credit stayed relatively quiet with Angela in her despair, if only for a while.

The chaplain then thinks to herself, "Angela has lost her spiritual center." (The meaning "spiritual center" is not exegeted.) Certainly Angela has lost the will to live. Certainly we can agree that Angela has experienced a horrifying life-altering blow at age 17, a blow from which she will likely never much recover, and as a result, it is not even clear that she will recover the will to live. What else does the chaplain need to know? And if Angela could find a "spiritual center" would her anguish be over?

The next phase of the relationship between Angela and the chaplain is full of discussion topics about the power of prayer, the power of God, whether God actually reached down and broke Angela's neck, or not, as well as the discussion of several biblical texts introduced by the chaplain. The chaplain is increasingly propelled into a catechetical mode. It's as if she were instructing a potential novice in the mysteries of the Christian faith. And the chaplain's lines in the verbatim sections become significantly longer than the patient's, usually an indicator of a chaplain's dysfunction. Pastoral counseling has collapsed and the chaplain has morphed into a catechist or propagandist. The chaplain says to the patient, for example: "I believe that God's will for us is always related to what is truly good for us, but that in the middle of a painful situation, especially one as painful as yours, it's hard to find the good. With time, though, we might see it."

Yes, perhaps. And with time we might *not* see it. My thought in first reading this was the wish to be able to send this Pollyanna chaplain down to the underworld to give that bit of pious wisdom to all the dead from Auschwitz. She could report back, "It's hard to see the good in those deaths, but we know it must be there, because God is good."

The chaplain, as pocket philosopher, has lost her way.

"Suffering is so hard to understand," says the chaplain, in a further display of banality. And then she expresses surprise and dismay that Angela thinks that God actually reached down and severed her spine. Why wouldn't Angela think that? Omnipotence means the power to do anything.

Discussions ensue as to whether God is responsible for the accident and injury. The chaplain seems to do most of the talking, and is very protective of God's innocence, as is typical of religious authorities.

Then in the midst of the sermonizing and religious education a ray of hope breaks in. Angela says, out of the blue, that it always helps when Josh visits. Josh is another rehab patient Angela's age who has similar injuries. Angela has found a new friend, one her age and in a predicament like her own. Then Angela asks the chaplain to assist her in blowing her nose, something she of course cannot do for herself. Angela cannot even hold a tissue. Next she asks the chaplain to wash her face, and afterward says, "That feels better, so much better. Thank you." We have the first recorded inkling of Angela's recovered will to live, faint as it may be. Angela dismisses the chaplain and asks that she return tomorrow. In her departure the chaplain of course feels the need to offer yet one more prayer.

In due course Angela is discharged to a long-term treatment center. Her family is unable to care for her and seemingly little interested. We never hear about her further.

## II.  The Published Critiques

The published critiques were quite weak.

The co-editor's (Steve Nolan) critique merely summarizes, adding nothing.

The psychologist critic (Sian Cotton) points out that the chaplain aims to "be a sign of God's incarnational love" and to help Angela establish a relationship with God that would "center and sustain her" in the future. He calls the chaplain's interventions and clinical choices "spot on." He also claims that the chaplain's "spiritual care transformed and assisted Angela." He does add, appropriately, that the chaplain might have explored Angela's parental abandonment, along with her other losses resulting from her accident. His one assertion, that I heartily concur with, was that this was "one of the most emotionally ... powerful" stories he has ever read. On balance, the psychologist critic failed in his assignment. He was far from "spot on."

The chaplain critic (Alister W. Bull) was the strongest of the three. He felt ambivalent about the religious focus that emerged in this case, as well as in the previous two cases. He charges that the chaplain often took the lead in introducing religious language and constructs with which they were familiar. I wish he had been less ambivalent and more direct; nevertheless I say, "Bravo to the chaplain critic!"

## III.  The Author's Perspective

Clinical pastoral criticism in the U.S., coming as it does out of the Boisen movement, is a tradition of strong clinical criticism. The critics in this case hardly qualify as strong. Except for the one offered by the chaplain critic, the critiques of this case were almost useless.

Overall, Angela's chaplain assumed too much of the role of God's little defense attorney. She should already know that that's a role, ever since Job, which no one should undertake under any circumstances. How could anyone defend the turning of a lively 17-year-old girl into a quadriplegic? Who would even want to? But who can put God in the dock? It's a case one cannot win.

The proper posture of a clinical chaplain is agnostic, regardless of the chaplain's own personal beliefs and allegiances. The clinical role demands it. In this era, chaplains present themselves to persons of many different faiths, and faiths within faiths, as well as persons of no faith at all. A proper clinician does not represent any specific religion or tradition if the chaplain wants to remain a clinician. Indoctrination and proselytizing do not belong in the clinical setting. The chaplain in this case was continually promoting her own pious beliefs. That is not acceptable.

I think we must be suspicious of the chaplain's cavalier dismissal of Angela's own congregational minister on the grounds that Angela didn't relate to him. Angela was in no condition to relate to anyone for much of her time in the hospital. Unless there are clear contra-indications—and there may be—the chaplain should encourage the connection between the minister and Angela. One visit can hardly be determinative. Angela has only meager support from her family. The chance that any minister might take an interest in her should be valued on its face. We have to be suspicious that discounting the minister is rooted in the half-millennium of hostility between Catholics and Protestants, and wonder in this case if the chaplain's own Catholicism was skewing her assessment of Angela's Protestant minister. The minister and the chaplain were, after all, in a competitive role during Angela's hospitalization. Suspicion is warranted.

The one point in the case that was clearly redemptive, in my view, was Angela's reporting that it always helps when the 17-year-old Josh, a quadriplegic like herself, comes to visit. *Mirabile dictu,* she has found a boy for a friend, a boy immobilized like her, and in that she has found, perhaps, even the will to live. Then she asked the chaplain to help her blow her nose and then to wash her face. "That feels better, so much better. Thank you," she said, and then asked the chaplain to return the next day. The quadriplegic 17-year-old Angela has found a will to live, if only for that moment. It's enough to make a grown man weep.

Buried in all the chaplain's religiosity and talkativeness, Angela must have sensed that there was a compassionate human being in there, human enough to be asked to blow her nose and wash her face.

This case demonstrates that we can be instruments of healing sometimes even when our skills abandon us and our awareness is dim. Perhaps it is a matter of simply being human, utterly human: blowing the nose and washing the face of a young quadriplegic girl who has just met a boy she likes.

I do conclude that the chaplain in this case was ultimately a blessing to Angela—but in spite of herself. It was a very close thing. The chaplain made a revelatory confession in her concluding paragraph, stating, "I entered Angela's darkness while keeping my eyes on the light of hope." This tells me that the chaplain's own counter transference was so strong that she could hardly bear staying focused on the patient. For her own protection—and sanity, perhaps—she piled high her religious teaching and her piety as a defense against the horror of Angela's predicament. But enough humanity seems to have broken through her anxiety, enabling the chaplain to reach Angela. Perhaps one day she will be able to do much more.

The fact that the chaplain in this case now is teaching other chaplains, as well as medical students and psychiatric residents, about the work of chaplaincy should sound the alarm to any who care about the profession. I do wish this chaplain would get into advanced clinical pastoral training that is psycho-dynamically oriented, in the Boisen tradition. Her heart seems to be right, but her practice is very much lacking.

I do wonder what eventually happened in Angela's life, and in Josh's. They are now in their mid-twenties. If they are alive. I fear the worst.

# CASE 4
# A Nigerian Immigrant in Britain Under the Spell of Witches

## I. The Case

Yesuto is a Nigerian man in his early thirties who has lived in England since he was 18. He is a psychiatric hospital patient, troubled because he believes he is under the spell of a Nigerian witch. He also has a history of depression and psychotic episodes. He calls himself a very bad Christian. He had stopped attending church, praying, and reading the Bible. "I am a sinner", he says, and "all my suffering deserved." He is full of self-condemnation, reports the chaplain. He is so frightened of witches that he cannot sleep.

The chaplain is a female Christian minister, who herself had emigrated from Bagdad, Iraq, as an infant. She was called in by the medical staff. "My name is Rosie," she says in introducing herself to the patient.

The chaplain counters Yesuto's feeling of being bewitched with those parts of the Bible that teach unconditional love and forgiveness. Yesuto says he had forgotten about those passages.

Yesuto's parents were currently visiting from Nigeria, and they were reinforcing Yesuto's beliefs in witchcraft. All this tension was exacerbated by the recent birth of his first child, a boy. Yesuto is fearful of what might happen to his son when he reaches age eight. The chaplain then asks what might have happened in Yesuto's own life at age eight. It turns out that Yesuto had been sent away to a boarding school at that age, a school where he was severely abused over an extended period of time.

The chaplain attempts to reassure Yesuto by suggesting that witches in Nigeria would not be able to work their craft from far away, and particularly through the walls of a psychiatric hospital.

The chaplain prayed a prayer of protection before she left, and visited him "three or four times more," with nothing important to report from those subsequent visits. In a matter of weeks Yesuto's fears dissipated and he was discharged.

The chaplain believed that warmth and open communication built trust in the relationship, leading to his recovery. Her approach was different from the medical staff that repeatedly told Yesuto that his beliefs were simply a symptom of his illness.

The chaplain reports that she follows the Rogerian philosophy of pastoral counseling. Later she says she resorted to cognitive behavioral therapy, focused on the here and now, and concentrated on introducing a different perspective to the patient. The impact, she reports, was an almost immediate improvement in his state of mind. "With a change of thoughts, there was a change in his feelings," she wrote. The last three weeks of visits with him "were centered mainly on Christian teaching.... I kept reinforcing the importance of focusing on love and acceptance," she wrote.

In conclusion the chaplain writes, "People's spiritual or religious beliefs should not be interpreted as symptoms of disordered minds."

## II.  The Published Critiques

The co-editor's (Steve Nolan) critique is very positive. This is a "particularly good example of the way an experienced chaplain is able, subtlety, (sic, meaning subtly), to use her knowledge and skills to therapeutic effect." Skillful listening, he says, is what she brings to the case; that is, "the person-centered approach of Carl Rogers and the skills of Socratic questioning as developed within cognitive behavioral therapy." He concludes that a significant proportion of what troubles Yesuto was sociocultural and religious rather than simply psychiatric, and that his psychiatric needs were being compounded by cultural misunderstanding on the part of his health caregivers." He gives the chaplain high marks for her knowledge, skills, and experience.

The chaplain/psychologist's (Graeme D. Gibbons) critique is gentle but substantive. He applauds the chaplain's empathetic interest in the patient. He applauds her astute question on hearing Yesuto's fear that his son would die when he reached his eighth year: "What happened to you when *you* were eight years old." The critic, though, gently chides the chaplain's claim to have focused on the here and now and for following a cognitive-behavioral therapy approach. He argues that she went beyond the cognitive-behavioral by dredging up his memories of being eight, and is happy she did. He suggests that Yesuto will not be much helped by logic and cognitive thinking. He recommends "empathetic understanding and responsiveness" by way of either long-term psychotherapy or support of a caring Christian community.

The psychiatrist critic (Warren Kinghorn) applauds the chaplain's general approach and her affirmation that religious and spiritual beliefs should not be interpreted as symptoms of disordered minds, even if sometimes they may be. He criticizes the medical staff for pathologizing Yesuto's religious experience and exacerbating his shame. He also points out that, paradoxically, the chaplain undermines her own position when she herself pathologized Yesuto's particular religious beliefs, citing them as detrimental to his mental well-being. And at that juncture, he points out, the chaplain became more directive and didactic, quoting various biblical texts that emphasize God's unconditional love. This effectively distanced her from the patient. While Yesuto does not in fact appear to have been distanced, he may have felt at that point that he had no option but to comply.

Kinghorn also expounds at length on the complex nature of the relationship between psychiatry and the work of religious clinicians. He writes: "It is not unthinkable—or, at least, should not be unthinkable—that a well-equipped chaplain might challenge a psychiatrist's core formulation of a particular patient's mental health problem." He argues that chaplains "play an exceedingly important role in attending to the humanistic gap created when bioscientific medical practices come into contact with the complex, context-constituted lives of people who are sick." And he calls into question whether any sharp distinction between the 'psychiatric' and the 'spiritual' is either necessary or tenable.

## III. The Author's Perspective

Not too many years have passed since witchcraft was widely believed to have been practiced in the U.S. and Europe, and the public responded with bloodbaths and burnings as alleged witches were arrested, brutally imprisoned, and often executed. The public in the Western world now seems to have moved on to other forms of irrationality and mostly have left the witches behind. But, they are now being found in Nigeria. It does seem, though, that current Nigerians are more forgiving and tolerant of their witches than Westerners were a few years back. We don't hear of burnings and killings of witches in Nigeria. Yet it seems that some Nigerians, and certainly this Nigerian, do have a similar kind of irrational fear of witches.

The chaplain's first burden here is to assess the personal meaning and significance of witchcraft, to determine what it means to the patient who feels he has been bewitched. I believe we can draw on the history of witchcraft generally. And one thing we can learn is that witchcraft is entirely a product of the imagination, undoubtedly with deep roots in the unconscious. In Western tradition witches were almost exclusively women, typically either aged women or young girls at or around puberty. Witchcraft had an unmistakable link to sexuality, particularly female sexuality. These associations might be useful in any effort to provide counseling to Yesuto.

It is noteworthy, too, that the outbreak of the hysteria over the sexual abuse of children during the last two decades of the 20th century carried occasional references to witchcraft. And certainly the hysteria over the sexual abuse of children was a social irruption with some of the same irrational dynamics of the earlier witch-hunts. While being unfamiliar with Nigerian culture, we can say with confidence that witchcraft in the Western world has clear links to sexuality and the unconscious.

All of which is to say that witchcraft should be treated as a problem in the mind, and thus a problem to be engaged by serious psychoanalytically informed counseling.

An appropriate pastoral counseling stance with Yesuto might be to begin with his thoughts and feelings about sexuality. We note that he is married and recently has become a father, both matters of sex. Marriage and fatherhood would likely lead to stress in his life—or anyone's life, for that matter. Being an African in Britain, given all the innuendoes about black sexuality in the context of white culture, would likely exacerbate any sexual anxiety he might be carrying. And his visiting parents, bearing their native superstition about witchcraft, undoubtedly added to any stress he may have been developing.

If this picture is accurate, what is called for is a sympathetic listening to Yesuto's account of all this ... listening, and as Freud proposed, making connections. As Yesuto expounds on his concerns he will likely find relief, especially if the chaplain disciplines herself and restrains from offering pious remedies and biblical teaching. Certainly the chaplain ought not suggest or even hint that she believes in the facticity of witches. She should avoid that argument altogether. Contrariwise, she *should* believe, of course, in the power of the unconscious mind and its power that is both to enrich us and to do us in.

The chaplain in this case vacillates between being a Rogerian, who was broadly in the psychoanalytic stream, and the cognitive-behavioral philosophy of counseling, which is quite mechanistic. As a result she checkmates herself.

As the chaplain/psychologist critic pointed out, she brilliantly connected Yesuto's fear of his son dying at age eight with Yesuto's own exile to a tortuous boarding school when he himself was eight. The chaplain was on track and going in the right direction. But she soon derailed herself, resorting to mini-lectures on the Bible, as the psychiatrist critic pointed out.

The chaplain's summary statement argues that "people's spiritual or religious beliefs should not be interpreted as symptoms of disordered minds." My rejoinder is, what's wrong with a disordered mind? There is probably no living being whose mind is not to some extent disordered. To focus on illness reduces persons to the level of their illness, she says. Yet anytime one consults a physician, one is focusing on illness. That's why we pay them. I suspect the chaplain may be covertly railing against the hospital staff and their cavalier treatment of Yesuto, in which case she could have simply said as much.

I am puzzled, or should I say more truthfully, troubled, by the chaplain's claim to "stand in (or represent) the space between this world and the next." She suggests that this space is the world of spirituality. The construct is troublesome fiction. Even as a metaphor it is troubling. Religious people have postulated "a next world," a metaphor that is of itself troubling enough, but possibly necessary even from a psychological perspective. Now this chaplain postulates yet another space, one between this world and the next, and it's where she proposes to position herself. This along with all the spirituality talk sounds increasingly like fanciful thinking.

It should be a matter of concern that the chaplain elected to present for review only the first of several of her visits to Yesuto, the implication being that nothing of note occurred in subsequent visits. This is counterintuitive, in that a developing relationship would tend to reach a higher level of significance as time passed. One has to wonder about the substance of the subsequent visits, and why they were presented as of no consequence to the relationship as a whole.

My major criticism of this case is that the chaplain seems never to have been exposed to serious clinical pastoral training. If she had been, she might have treated Yesuto's fears of witchcraft as part of his troubled interior life.

Freud gave up hypnotism because changing one's cognition is not the same as a deep understanding of one's inner conflicts. Cognitive-behavioral therapy undoubtedly works sometime, like hypnotism. In the tradition of the clinical pastoral training movement, self-understanding trumps behavioral adjustment.

And I do not think the chaplain helps the therapeutic process by introducing herself as "Rosie." Such an introduction creates a contrived hint of intimacy that undermines her role as one who might guide Yesuto in a journey toward a stronger sense of self. Given the fact that the chaplain is a white woman, any such innuendo of intimacy could very well exacerbate Yesuto's panic, rooted as it seems to be in sexuality.

On balance, however, it could be that Yesuto actually benefited from the ministrations of the chaplain, probably, in part, because at least she was sympathetic and encouraging. Perhaps she was even the anti-witch. And unlike the other clinical staff, she did not simply declare Yesuto to be crazy, which is hardly therapeutic. However, she could have done so much more for him had she followed up on her curiosity about the content of Yesuto's imaginings, such as attention to the age-eight parallel. And she would have done better had she laid aside the biblical instruction and other cognitive-behavioral approaches. She then might have spent more time listening to the complicated array of Yesuto's concerns and assisting him in making connections. The poignant fact here is that the chaplain's kind-heartedness might well have led to a significantly therapeutic relationship with Yesuto had the chaplain been more clinically oriented. Thus, though we do not know what ultimately happened in Yesuto's life, the story here might be either one of the triumph of human kindliness or the failure of a chaplain whose training is unfinished.

# CASE 5
# A Feisty British Woman Veteran Is Ready To Die

## I. The Case

June is a 78-year-old British woman with emphysema who, in a very methodical way, attempted suicide. Prior to taking her lethal overdose of medication, she wrote a letter to the local police station notifying them of her action so that they would be the ones to find her body. Due to unfortunate planning, her letter arrived too quickly. The police found her unconscious but still alive and transported her to the hospital where she was resuscitated. Her first response on regaining consciousness was anger. Soon thereafter she requested to see "a padre."

June was a spunky woman. Her first question to the chaplain was, "Are you a chaplain or a God-botherer?" She explained that in her years in the Royal Air Force the chaplains assigned to their units were always classified (unofficially, of course) as one or the other. She was not interested in a "God-botherer."

In retrospect June seems like someone who would be a pleasure to be around. She is direct, candid, and outspoken. She is neither a clinging vine nor a wilting violet.

June tells the chaplain of the circumstances of her attempted suicide. She had been in an intimate relationship with another woman who had recently died, leaving June with nothing to live for, wishing only to join her friend in death. She asks the chaplain if God will keep them apart in the afterlife. While he dodges the question somewhat, and no one can blame him for that, he does assure her that God is a loving God. She goes on further to complain that the staff has access to her notification letter to the police, have been laughing at the document, and laughing as well at the fact that she loved another woman.

June and her lover had no friends; they hardly knew the neighbors. The day her lover died she drove to a church and prayed. She now feels that she has nothing left to live for. She and her lover had visited some churches recently but never found what they were looking for. The chaplain asks whether communion was something important to her. She says it had been, some time back. He inquires whether she would like to receive it while in the hospital. She would like that, she says, and the chaplain follows up.

On the third visit, June tells of her dilemma. She is facing an assessment meeting by the hospital staff. If she tells the staff that she intends to repeat the suicide attempt, as she has confided to the chaplain that she so intends, they will not release her. "Do I lie and get my freedom, or tell the truth and be kept locked up?" she asks. "I will lie," she says. Will the chaplain accompany her to the review committee meeting? The chaplain is the only person she knows to ask to accompany her. "I'm not asking you to say anything; just to be there. I'd find it helpful to have you there with me. Would you do that?" The chaplain agrees. She passes muster without the chaplain having to say anything.

June next asked that the chaplain make contact with her local parish so as to make it easy for her to be connected when she gets home. He follows up, notifying the parish as requested. When she is released, however, the chaplain begins to fret over whether he will hear that she has killed herself. He hears nothing.

The next contact the chaplain has with June is a year-and-a-half later, on Christmas day. He is called to the hospital, following June's written directive, to find June in intensive care, unconscious. She died a few hours later. The reader is not told whether she committed suicide or died of her progressive emphysema. Nor do we know anything about her possible relationship with the parish during her 18 months of life following her earlier hospitalization.

# II. The Published Critiques

The editor's (Steve Nolan) critique merely summarizes the case.

The chaplain-psychologist's (Graeme D. Gibbons) critique first challenges the cultural environment that understands suicide only as an act of alienation, to be opposed at every opportunity. And he supposes that the chaplain provided June with a confirmatory relationship that finally enabled her to go on living, at least for a while. But he wished the chaplain had been a little stronger about what he felt and where he stood. He wished the chaplain had said something like:

"June, I think this is one area of belief that parts of the church have in the past got seriously wrong. I believe you have experienced the loss of someone whose value has been extremely important to you. You were in deep despair, and one of the ways people try to escape from despair is to try foolishly to make it right themselves, to take it on themselves. That act is often a cry for help. I would like to work with you to try to understand how important it is for you to join your friend, even if that means later you try to complete what you didn't succeed with this time. I would like you and me to be clear about your love of this woman, a love that is so powerful."

The psychiatrist critic (Warren Kinghorn) affirmed the chaplain's resolve not to go 'prospecting' for reasons why June should not choose to die. He also pointed out that the chaplain communicated significant pastoral care through his clerical role, listening to her without judgment and delivering her the Holy Communion as well as the hand off of June to a local parish. But he also suggests that the hand off lacked follow up. Furthermore, he notes that the chaplain's decision not to disclose to the medical staff June's ongoing thoughts of attempting suicide again was a missed opportunity for all. Had June's actual posture been shared with all, the potential enlightenment for everyone might have been very significant. The problem is, as the psychiatrist points out, that moving in that direction would potentially threaten the chaplain's own relationship with June, unless she could be persuaded fully to join such a project. Moreover, the chaplain might be gambling his own professional position in the hospital if the full-disclosure route unraveled in any way. But the psychiatrist is correct that the potential benefits of full and candid disclosure might have been very edifying to everyone concerned.

When I reflect back and wonder how courageous I might have been in one of my hospital positions had I faced this particular dilemma, I don't know what I might have done. I would like to think I would have had the courage to attempt what the psychiatrist proposes. I also know that clergy living on family trusts tend to have more courage to take such risks than those living from paycheck to paycheck.

## III. The Author's Perspective

I am not much persuaded by the chaplain/psychologist's critique. It seems he wants to open discussion with June about suicide and homosexuality. Interesting subjects of discussion as they might be, my impression is that the salient issue for June is her isolation and lack of community.

I concur most strongly with the psychiatrist's assessment and criticism. But I want to single out and highlight his suggestion that the chaplain failed to follow through on his referral to the local parish on June's behalf. Certainly June's central predicament was social isolation, partly driven of course by her late sexually deviant relationship, and more significantly, the death of her lover. The purpose of the church, or any reputable religious community, is to build a caring community committed to human values. June was left in the care of the local parish. But was there any follow up? Did the pastor there care enough to look in on her? Did the congregation care enough to embrace her, or was it the more typical gathering of sheep without a vision of caring for the ones lost and socially adrift?

It is heart-rending to think that June may well have lived her last 18 months in a replay of the kind of social isolation that she experienced since the death of her lover. One could argue that any blame is on her, that she and her lover elected to be isolates. But that is an evasion. I say that the chaplain, and the religious community at large probably (almost certainly) failed June in her last years, both before and after her lover died. It would not have taken a great amount of time and energy for the chaplain to call the attention of June's parish to her need, and even to have been overbearing in his referral, communicating that June was one of God's children, so to speak, and that she was being neglected in her time of greatest need. Sometimes one needs to become aggressive with lazy clergy and uncaring congregations.

Or could it be that this Anglican chaplain thinks that communion is bread and wine piously delivered, that he is not aware that real communion is the mutual relationships of care among persons in a loving and obedient community?

The distinguishing feature of pastoral care that makes it different from scientifically based psychiatry is its vision of restoring the whole human community. The shepherd leaves the ninety-nine to attend to the one lost sheep. While this is a Christian parable, it is actually a parable of any religion worthy of the name religion. June was a lost sheep. Terminally ill. Marked as a sexual outcast. Without family. Bereft of any significant human attachment. The shepherd abandoned her, and went off to care for the ninety-nine. It is painful to contemplate—without knowing anything for sure—what June's remaining 18 months may have been like after the chaplain abandoned her with a courtesy call to the local parish.

The chaplain was undoubtedly a blessing to June, which is almost certainly why she left instructions for him to be called at her time of death. But he went only halfway to the well.

This case is mainly a study on the failure of society at large. More particularly it is a case about the failure of the religious community, specifically the Church in this case, for its inattention to the sexually deviant among us, and its carelessness in relation to the marginalized in general, such as, the aged, the friendless, and members of racial minorities. It's a story all too common.

# CASE 6

# A Young Man Conflicted Over Sexual Identity

## I. The Case

Nate is a 20-year-old Dominican male admitted to an inpatient psychiatric ward after a suicide attempt, ingesting a large amount of acetaminophen and ibuprofen. With flat affect, he said that everything in his life had been terrible. He admitted struggling with his sexual identity, specifically his homosexuality, adding that he was "only a little bit like that." He was fearful that disclosure would result in complete rejection by his family and his Dominican community. There were two previous equally halfhearted suicide attempts.

On admission to the psychiatric unit, a spiritual screening was performed by nursing staff. One of the questions was whether the patient would like to see a chaplain. The chaplain in this institution was also an immigrant, from Germany, and a woman. It is not stated how he answered that question.

On his first day on the ward, Nate requested a Bible and the chaplain delivered it. When the chaplain arrived, Nate denied having made such a request. The chaplain apologized and offered to return the Bible, but he told her to leave it on the desk, that it wouldn't do any harm. The chaplain then told him that some patients find religion or spirituality helpful and others found it to be a source of struggle. What kind of person was he, the chaplain asked? He needed to rest, he said. He did agree that she could return another day.

They met a few days later. Nate was guarded and uneasy, but soon disclosed that he was feeling much better. He shared some of the conflict he was having with his family, without mentioning sexual issues. He discussed plans for moving out of his current living quarters provided him by his mother's cousin. He disclosed how close he was to his mother. The chaplain referred to this as a trust-building visit.

On the day of his discharge, on a chance meeting in the hallway, Nate asked the chaplain to call a Roman Catholic priest. According to policy the chaplain asked what specific sacramental need was involved. Nate stated that his family wanted him to see a priest for confession.

Now the chaplain felt she faced an ethical dilemma. She felt called upon to engage Nate in an attempt "to find an alternate way of constructing a meaningful spiritual/religious orientation." She wanted him to find ways to make autonomous choices regarding his religious practices. The dialogue was reported as follows:

Nate: (embarrassed, fidgety, unsteady eye contact) Yes, I want to do the confession/absolution thing. You know, I think it might be a good idea before I leave here.... Well, it is really more my family who wants me to see a priest. I mean I am okay going along with it.... I mean it can't hurt, right?

Chaplain: Well, I am happy to call a Roman Catholic priest, if this is your request.... But I don't think it's a good idea if you call a priest because your family wants you to see a priest.

Twice more Nate says he'll just go along with his family's wish, and the chaplain responds, suggesting Nate lacks autonomy. Then the following:

Chaplain: I'll tell you what.... How about you tell them that you had a conversation with the chaplain on the unit, who is an ordained pastor of the Lutheran Church. You could say that you got to talk about everything that needed to be talked about, that the conversation took about 45 minutes, and that it was meaningful to you.

Nate: (surprised) You are a real pastor?

Chaplain: Yes. Master of Divinity, ordination, the whole nine yards!

Nate: (smiling) Sounds like a plan.... I mean I don't feel like I need a priest. They just want me to do that.

Chaplain: So, how about we talk and make it a conversation that is meaningful to you.

The conversation continues. The subjects discussed were Nate's plans for living quarters, separating from the current close association with family members, his homosexual identity and his family's extreme aversion to homosexuality, and whether it really is a sin to act on homosexual desires.

Nate: I think I am really gay. I mean, I think about guys. I am attracted to guys. That's just how it is for me.

Chaplain: Yes, this is how God made you. And God loves you the way you are.

Nate then returns to discussing his family, and finally talks about how he needs to move beyond the restraints of family. Nate appears to relax.

Chaplain: Do you ever talk to God about any of this?

Nate: Not so much. But I say my prayers. And I am a Eucharistic minister.

Chaplain: The practices of the Roman Catholic Church are important to you?

Nate: Yes. And I pray.

Chaplain: (pause) Would you like for us to say a prayer together?

Nate: (appearing more withdrawn) Yes.

Chaplain: We don't have to.

Nate: No, I think it would be OK to say a prayer.

Chaplain: What are you praying for as you leave here today?

Nate: (solemnly, looking down) For me to keep taking my medication and to go see the therapist.

Chaplain: To take your medication and to see your therapist.

Nate: And to stay on track with what the team told me to do.

Chaplain: And to stay on track. Anything else?

Nate: No, that's about it.

The chaplain prays and blesses Nate. There was no further recorded contact.

In staff discussion the hospital psychiatrist reported a revelatory statement made by Nate himself: "Look, I am sitting in this chair. The chair is my family, my religion, my culture, and my community. You are asking me to join these people over there that are more like me. But you do not understand. If I do this, I have to leave my chair."

## II. The Published Critiques

The co-editor critic (Steve Nolan) pointed out that the chaplain places a high value on autonomy. He also pointed out that the chaplain is more directive than most, but he did not venture to offer an opinion on the effectiveness or appropriateness of such direction.

The chaplain/psychologist critic (Graeme D. Gibbons) was very positive about both the chaplain's assessment and of her work. He appreciated the care and patience the chaplain invested in helping Nate make his own decision about calling or not calling a priest. And he affirmed the way the chaplain opened up the issue of human sexuality by describing it as being on a continuum from hetero- to homosexuality.

The psychiatrist critic (Warren Kinghorn) challenged the chaplain's decision to discourage Nate from calling for a Catholic priest. He says it was understandable, in that Nate's gesture toward suicide was driven in part by his religion. But the psychiatrist calls this a missed opportunity for Nate to engage more deeply his Catholic faith while within the safety zone of the inpatient unit. Catholicism is the "chair" Nate sits in, capturing his own words, and his place is mediated by family values and history. As the psychiatrist says, "Why not, then, allow Nate to meet with the priest and for the chaplain to remain available to process that engagement with him, with a possible subsequent conversation with the priest also?" The psychiatrist also cautions that the priest might refer Nate to reparative therapy, a program that would aim to change his sexual desire patterns and restore him to heterosexuality. Were that to occur, however, the medical team would have firm grounds for challenging the priest, since such programs overstate the scientific consensus on such alleged therapy.

The psychiatrist also challenged the chaplain's assertion, regarding Nate's homosexuality, that "this is how God made you." He points out that the research literature is not so clear. Sexual orientation and identity is a complex form of the human experience developed within interconnected matrices of biology, environment, and culture. And sexual identity, though stable for most, is for others fluid over time. "It is better, then," he writes, "for both clinicians and religious authorities to walk alongside people like Nate with epistemological and moral humility, providing support and care in the context of deeply personal journeys without subsuming them into any preexisting cultural scripts."

## III. The Author's Perspective

This is the only case among those nine in the book that explicitly follows the co-editor's (George Fitchett) proposed Spiritual Assessment Tool, which he calls "Seven by Seven." Fitchett proposes that cases demonstrate seven areas of exploration: medical, psychological, psychosocial, family systems, ethnic and cultural, societal, and spiritual. Following that, seven dimensions should be explored: beliefs and meaning, vocation and consequences, experience and emotion, courage and growth, ritual and practice, community, and authority and guidance. Supplementing that, the chaplain in this particular case also draws on Kenneth Pargament's positive and negative religious coping regimen. The religious coping regimen includes the search for meaning, intimacy with others, identity, control, anxiety reduction, transformation, and the search for the sacred or spirituality itself. And it involves behaviors, emotions, relationships, and cognitions.

The checklist of Fitchett's fourteen and Pargament's seven items seem both redundant and externalistic, detached from the patient himself. The attention given to the topics in the lists do not help much in clarifying Nate's predicament nor in suggesting a way forward.

Each of the 20 or so topics represents areas of attention that might be important in a given case, and, thus, might be worthy of examination. But reliance on the lists distracts from focusing on the patient as a singular and idiosyncratic human being.

It seems that Fitchett's Spiritual Assessment Tool, as well as Pargament's, is a distraction from the aims of effective pastoral care and counseling. The chaplain's burden is to listen, with a third ear, so to speak, for the heart of the matter in an encounter with a patient. The burden of a 14-point or 21-point focus tends to reduce the chaplain to a surveyor or a collector of data. Certainly we seek data, but we seek it in order to understand the riddle of the life of another. Pastoral care and counseling is a subtle art that is undermined by an impulse for data collecting.

I suspect that the extensive checklist that the chaplain relies on was a distraction and drew the chaplain away from the primary task of counseling, that of understanding the patient. This may explain why the chaplain's attempts to change the patient obscured the task of understanding him. As the chaplain writes, "Shame and self-deprecation were countered with the assurance of God's love for God's creation (*i.e.*, Nate himself)." The chaplain elects to preach Nate to a resolution of his sexual and religious conflict. Similarly, the chaplain believed that she had empowered Nate in offering him an experience of simply talking to God in human ways, a new way to pray. Religious manipulation is simply an extension of behavior modification. That the chaplain wished for Nate to find a religious home that would not condemn him for his homosexual feelings is understandable and caring, but it is ill informed. Her manipulativeness is incongruent with the standard of practice in the clinical pastoral field.

Strangely enough, the hospital psychiatrist's report portrays Nate as being quite aware of his predicament. The chaplain's Nate and the psychiatrist's Nate hardly appear to be the same person. Nate says, as reported by the psychiatrist, "Look, I'm sitting in this chair.... You are asking me to join those people over there...." To do so, Nate says he would have to leave the chair he sits in, the world to which he belongs. It is a very poignant and insightful confession on Nate's part of his predicament. That suggests that the psychiatrist and the chaplain, as well as other staff, would have done well to pool their impressions of

Nate and attempt to reach a consensus on who he was and how to treat him. Seemingly nothing of the sort took place.

The chaplain's philosophy of religion (and spirituality), as something that some find helpful and others not, seems to derogate religion to the category of utility, something to be picked up and used, or not. Serving in a public institution, chaplains would do better to promote a more universal definition of religion, namely as whatever value and belief system that the patient holds and which offers meaning. When the chaplain invites Nate to consider talking to God, she is proselytizing for a particular religious posture, and one that is apparently alien to him. Some religious persons would consider "talking to God" *prima facie* absurd.

Warren Kinghorn's consultation is brilliant in pointing out that more might be gained by tolerating Nate's proposed meeting with the priest, with the chaplain waiting in a potential consultant's role. He also chides the chaplain, correctly, for her assurance to Nate that God made him homosexual. As Kinghorn suggests, we know from prison history, and other social constructs, that a significant portion of the population is quite malleable and changeable as regards sexual identity.

I would add too, that the chaplain seemed to be promoting her own well-intentioned agenda, namely her advocacy for an oppressed sub-group, homosexuals. Admirable as it is to stand in solidarity with oppressed minorities, the proper role of pastoral care and counseling is to promote the personal empowerment of such oppressed persons. Leading them by the nose, so to speak, or pressuring them to act in a certain way hardly empowers. The chaplain is of course correct, that practicing homosexuals generally will be more welcome in certain other churches than the Catholic Church. But Kinghorn was correct, that the chaplain was too aggressive in her effort to get Nate to receive as an alternative her own Protestant blessing. As he wrote, her pressure prevented the possibility of other good things from occurring.

We should also note, however, that apparently the hospital psychiatrist (as opposed to the psychiatrist critic) also pressured Nate to own up to his homosexuality and change his community, or as Nate put it, to change from the chair in which he was sitting.

The chaplain's Protestant aggression in this case brings to mind the frequent question raised in group relations theory, namely, "What does this behavior unconsciously represent in the group (the hospital) as a whole?" One possibility is the chaplain's need to declare her own public solidarity with the homosexual subgroup. Such political involvement may be useful to society at large, but it also skews the chaplain's role in the institution where she works. Another possibility is that she is signaling her concurrence with the hospital psychiatrist, who also made an effort to move Nate out of his chair. A third possibility, more cosmic, is that the chaplain is firing one more latter-day salvo in the half-millennium conflict between Protestants and Catholics. Perhaps all three of these covert dynamics are at work here. Either one of these agendas is a distraction from the problem at hand—namely, the personal struggle of Nate to find a way to live as a self-authenticating person. He is already burdened heavily by those around him to shape himself to their own vision of him, which is, a good Catholic, heterosexual, obedient Dominican national, and who knows what else. He does not need more pressure from the chaplain, or the psychiatrist.

Chaplaincy as a public office today in this culture is dependent on benign good will among the multitudinous religions. The various religions are very much in competition, which is quite evident when one pulls back the cordial public mask. Any religious group that feels undercut or demeaned by another might set off an uproar, with the potential to disrupt the existing public comity that generally marks chaplaincies everywhere. Thus, I believe that the chaplain's proposal in this case, to stand in as a Catholic priest equivalent in relation to Nate, was ill-advised politically and the kind of gesture that could lead potentially to a great deal of mischief.

In my fantasy I imagine the trouble the chaplain might have been in had Nate said, "Hey, I like your kind of religion. When can I leave the Catholic Church and join the Lutherans?"

And another thing: What is the nursing department doing making spiritual assessments at the time of admission to this institution? If anyone can do this job, why do chaplains need all this training and credentialing? We cannot fault the chaplain for this, but it's an indication of the trouble that professionals trained in clinical pastoral care and counseling currently face—namely, the illusion that most anyone, trained or untrained, is an expert in spirituality and, therefore, can do the job.

Finally, I want to challenge the chaplain on her introductory statement to Nate: "Some patients [find] religion or spirituality helpful and others [find] it to be a source of struggle." This statement seems to characterize religion (and spirituality) as some kind of *thing* that one can pick up or put down, as needed, something on the order of an object, even an alien object. A more sophisticated definition of religion is whatever gives ultimate meaning and purpose to one's life. And I presume spirituality might mean the same if we ever are able to pin the word down.

# CASE 7
# A Canadian Veteran at the End of His Life

## I. The Patient

Andrew was a 91-year-old veteran with vascular dementia and cancer who has lived eight years on the cognitive support unit in a veterans' hospital. The chaplain is sure that "Andrew is capable of having a unique relationship with God." Two chaplains, one Anglican and one Catholic, care for him in a veterans' health center in Canada, though the former seems to have principal administrative authority. The patient is Catholic.

Anglican Chaplain: How is life treating you?

Andrew: I have had a good day, but I slept most of it away (chuckling).

Anglican Chaplain: What is making today so good?

Andrew: I spent time praying.

After a couple more exchanges:

Anglican Chaplain: Would you find a prayer meaningful to you right now?

Andrew: I sure would.

Anglican Chaplain prays, "... Amen."

Andrew: Oh boy, that was nice. (A large grin came to his face, and he laughed.)

Two weeks later:

Anglican Chaplain: Hi Andrew. It's the chaplain to see you.

Andrew: (mumbling something, and then in a whispery voice) I feel closer.

Anglican Chaplain: Closer to whom, Andrew?

Andrew: Closer to my father.

Anglican Chaplain: Do you mean closer to your father, God?

He nods.

Andrew's only daughter, Lee, calls to talk with the chaplain. The Anglican Chaplain refers Lee to the Catholic Chaplain because Lee had requested Catholic ministrations for her father at the end of his life. Lee describes herself as not actively religious.

Lee was nervous about talking with a priest, and she insisted that their first conversation be by phone. She was "concerned about how things might come out in the presence of a priest." She expressed feelings of deep isolation.

This was followed by an unscheduled office visit to the Catholic chaplain. She simply dropped by and found the chaplain available. She "spoke from her heart about how her father's decline was affecting her," writes the chaplain. She confessed that she was not a practicing Catholic, but turned to her faith in times of crisis. (Doesn't this make her some sort of "rice Christian"?)

Lee described her father as a wonderful loving man with no faults except for being too wonderful. She says, "He had faith in me." She was tearful. She disclosed that she was a hippie in her early years. "Maybe my father wasn't as caught up with me doing the right thing as much as he was making sure that I didn't have to face things alone. After all, I found myself in some real messes, and he said that we would get through it." She spoke of her father in idealized terms, and was unchallenged by the chaplain. And she claimed that she knows that his love for her will never die, that she will always have that. While no one need challenge such feelings, how much they are worth in the market is anyone's guess. It is noteworthy, however, that none of Andrew's foibles or faults are named, even in humor. It seems that in her father we are dealing with some kind of idealized figure.

At the close of the session, Lee and the chaplain have a laugh over her hippie past? "Did it surprise you that I was a hippie?" she asks him.

The Catholic chaplain and Lee next met for a second face-to-face counseling session; Lee was again tearful. The circumstance was the medical report that her father is no longer responding to treatment. The thrust of the discussion throughout was about how loving a father Andrew had been, and how deep her feelings of isolation are now that he is dying. "I can never be ready for this. I can't abandon him to death. What am I supposed to do?" The Catholic chaplain writes that Lee's spiritual struggle was the question of how faith and trust could see her through the devastating anguish of losing her father. She seems to have trouble letting her father die, but it is never clarified what that might be about. The chaplain exhibits no curiosity about this, and certainly does not broach any such curiosity with Lee. Her father has been on a downhill ride for eight years, and there can't be much more life left in him.

The chaplain's fourth contact was a scheduled anointing of Andrew. Andrew himself was not responsive, but neither was he struggling. He was close to death. Lee had prevailed upon her brother, Ed, to join the rite. The two chaplains speak at the anointing as well as various staff persons. Andrew is peaceful but not responsive. In the context of that gathering, the Catholic chaplain offers Ed his spiritual services. Ed does not take up the offer.

The two chaplains claim to engage in what they refer to as "deep listening." Deep listening does not seem to include suspicion or curiosity, the litmus test of competent counseling.

It is claimed that the Anglican chaplain enabled Andrew to feel supported in his connectedness with God, though it is not spelled out what such a connection might mean to Andrew or anyone else.

Upon Andrew's death, the Anglican chaplain conducted a bedside flag ceremony of his own design, a nonreligious tribute designed to honor veterans. The Canadian flag was draped over the body while family, friends, and staff paid tribute to his service to country. I found myself wondering what kind of honor would be presented to the pacifists, refuseniks, or conscientious objectors of recent wars who might happen to die at that particular facility. Perhaps they would not have been allowed through the door of the hospital.

The case contains no data about any Catholic funeral rites, which we must presume took place.

## II.  The Published Critiques

The co-editor critic (Steve Nolan) applauds the two chaplains as "models of tenderness and compassion—the love that transforms mere ritual into authentic spiritual care." He states that the Catholic chaplain demonstrates listening skill with real subtlety, preferring to call it "deep listening"; what some counselors/therapists call *advanced empathy*.

The chaplain critic (David Mitchell) makes the argument that since it is now understood that religion is different from spirituality, chaplaincy can claim its roots in religion, all within the larger category of spirituality. And of course all of it is evidence-based. The critic also wonders if more could have been done for Andrew's son, Ed, who has been on the fringe of the decline, death, and burial activities. But then he adds that not going down that road with Lee paid dividends. What the dividends might have been is not stated. The chaplain critic also wonders if the wider medical team were aware of the depth of the work of the two chaplains, suggesting that they probably were not.

The nurse critic (Barbara Pesut) is generally positive. She states that the Anglican chaplain's "thank you" in response to Andrew's sharing of "his feeling of the presence of God a mark of ultimate respect." She calls it the beautifully acknowledged reciprocity of two individuals who stand in the presence of God. She also applauds the chaplain for his humor and mutual laughter when Andrew's daughter Lee reveals that she had been a hippie. The critic makes the judgment that Lee was engaged in a struggle common to people of faith— namely, how to treat her dying and finally deceased father.

# III. The Author's Perspective

A considerable amount of conventional religious piety is embedded in both this case and the three critiques. Very little clinical astuteness is in evidence in either. I will comment only on select aspects of it.

I am not clear why the Anglican chaplain felt the need to put words in Andrew's mouth, as described in the initial exchange. When the dying Andrew says that he feels closer to his father, the Anglican chaplain responds, "Do you mean closer to your father, God?" Andrew nods yes. How could he say "no"? This exchange captures the troubling posture in general of both chaplains in this case. Each seems bent on soothing and pacifying—and closing doors—and neither seems to possess the suspicious eye of a trained clinician. Anton Boisen, long ago capturing the essence of the clinical posture, famously said, "It's not what the minister says to the boy, but what the boy says to the minister." Thus, in this case, what the chaplain says to Andrew is neither interesting nor useful. The proper clinical focus is on the non-verbal communication as well as the words of Andrew and Lee, and Ed. Both these chaplains demonstrate deafness to non-verbal communication. Furthermore, they failed to attend to the complexity and mystery of idiosyncratic communication.

Just how much Andrew is "with it" is not clear. Even if his senility is extreme, I do not see why the chaplain needs to speak *for* him, something he seems very quick to do. If Andrew is only marginally deficient mentally, even less does the chaplain need to speak for him. Whatever Andrew's mental status is, the chaplain seems bent on imposing himself and his words on the patient.

The Anglican chaplain also expresses concern about whether Andrew might be able to have a relationship with God in his current demented state, what he infelicitously refers to as "connectedness with God." I find this metaphor of connectedness both theologically inept and something of a wild goose chase. Relationship with God has always been one of those metaphors situated in the world of the imagination. Since God rarely, if ever, actually talks, it cannot be clear what the metaphor "relationship with God" might mean.

"Relationship" typically connotes mutual communication between two beings. A clinician would be hard pressed to demonstrate that the God-man "relationship" includes mutual communication.

A hermeneutics of suspicion ought to be in play even in a nursing home; or, perhaps, especially in a nursing home, where death walks the halls. Many suspicions arise out of this initial exchange between the Anglican chaplain and the patient. Sleeping, praying, and laughing are not a persuasive trio of a typical deathbed routine, even a slow-deathbed routine. The sleeping part I grasp, especially under the influence of medication. Praying perhaps, and yet this patient may well be tossing prayer sops the chaplain's way. Surely he knows what the chaplain wants to hear by now. And the patient's laughter seems distinctly out of joint subsequent to a prayerful appeal to the Almighty. Senility may of course be determinative here. It is hard to tell. Yet, the patient is not so senile that he seems unaware of what most pleases the chaplain, namely praying and meditating on God. Andrew's response to the chaplain's prayer, instead of his own "amen," has the faint sound of mockery, "Oh boy, that was nice," with a large grin and a laugh.

It also is puzzling that Lee does not venture into the possible meaning of her brothers extraordinary distance from this entire family drama. Nor does the chaplain inquire about the possible meaning of this behavior. Ed is prevailed upon to attend the final bedside anointing, along with various nurses and staff. Other than that, Ed is a ghostly figure. Such a stark fact within the family nexus requires a pastoral clinician to inquire about it. Certainly there is a story here behind Ed's distance from his sister and father, and his lack of response to the Catholic chaplain's offer of spiritual services. And certainly Lee knows the story, but the chaplain's lack of curiosity or initiative results in the secret being withheld from the counselor, and missing from the case.

The Catholic chaplain holds two face-to-face counseling sessions with Lee, subsequent to an initial phone session and prior to the anointing. The content of the sessions, as reported by the chaplain, seem vaguely contrived and seductive. In both private sessions Lee weeps. Her stated issue is whether she should let her father go. But he is virtually "gone" already, so her options are not options at all. Or, perhaps she means that *emotionally* she cannot release him. But that distinction is not made.

The counseling sessions are entirely driven by Lee and focused on Lee herself in relation to her father, with minimal investment on the part of the chaplain. At the end of a session, Lee offers some playful, sexually provocative innuendo about her earlier life as a hippie. "Did it surprise you that I was a hippie?" and they both laugh. It's not clear exactly what was funny. At the end of the next session Lee says, "I found myself in some real messes ... my father wasn't as caught up with me doing the right thing as much as he was making sure that I didn't have to face things alone...." Clearly Lee is a woman who has not let life pass her by, and has tested some boundaries, but it seems that the Catholic chaplain doesn't really want to hear about such things.

Yet another dimension of this case that was unexplored is the incongruent nature of Lee's religious posture. She describes herself as not religious, and yet she communicates quite the contrary in her four conversations with the priest. Reading the accounts of her communications with the Catholic chaplain, we should conclude she is a more or less believing Catholic who simply has not been recently active, a far cry from her self-description at the onset of the relationship. Initially, she presented herself as non-religious and committed only to fulfilling her father's last wishes.

Each of the chaplains in this case was hobbled by a lack of theological depth, a lack of clinical seriousness, and a lack of curiosity. They communicate to the patient the message that they want to hear only the good news, or a positive spin on things. They fail to understand that the counselor's task is to hear the negative material, to hear the bad news, so to speak. Anyone can listen to good news. They signal to the patient, subtly and not so subtly, that they want to hear the positive, the upbeat, and the good news. They want to hear about faith and love, not doubt, hatred, or conflict.

Perhaps it is not too late for these two chaplains. They had the courage to display their intimate work for all the world to see, warts and all. Now it is time for them to take courage and educate themselves theologically and clinically.

# CASE 8
# David, a Mature Man Dying of Pancreatic Cancer

## I. The Case

The chaplain is a conservative rabbi, a woman born and raised in Germany, who took academic studies in the U.S., trained in nursing and chaplaincy, and is a board certified chaplain with the National Association of Jewish Chaplains. She volunteered for service in a hospital in Israel, in a poor and mixed area of Jews, Christians, and Muslims, where it seems most people come to die rather than for a cure. This is no state-of-the-art modern medical center.

The patient, David, is a 60-something Jewish patient with terminal pancreatic cancer. He grew up in the Old City. At age 16, he was summoned to the morgue to identify his mother's body after she was killed in a bombing. His father committed suicide soon thereafter, and David was left to care for his younger siblings and to run his father's business as a cobbler.

Though a patient, David seemed to have had the run of the hospital, so the chaplain at first assumed he was a family member of some sort. He did seem to enjoy following the medical staff around and intruding himself into situations where he did not belong. He paid little attention to boundaries of any sort.

The chaplain's first encounter with David went as follows:

Chaplain: Hi David, I'm Nina.

David: (looking at me quizzically) And who would you be? What can you do for me?

Chaplain: I am the *tomekhet rucharnit* ("supporter of the soul/spirit" in Hebrew, and the Hebrew title for "chaplain") here, and I thought you might want someone to talk to.

David: Spiritual...you mean like religion?

Chaplain: Yes, that is one part of what I do. I have time to listen, and if you would like, we can pray together.

David: Ahh, nonsense, religion is bad. Don't you see what it has done to this country, to all of us?

He spat on the floor, hit the wall with his fist, and left without even looking at me, reports the chaplain.

The chaplain goes on to stalk the patient (not in any negative sense, but more in "the hound of heaven" sense) over the next weeks. She often positioned herself near the coffee and tea station, and David sometimes would show up. For a while, neither words nor even eye contact were shared.

Returning after a long weekend absence, the chaplain received word from a nurse that David was looking for her with some urgency, and was on the balcony. The chaplain found him there.

David: I do not like to talk to people.

Chaplain: I could tell.

David: And I still don't like to.

Chaplain: You don't have to. (silence) But you shout pretty well for someone who does not like to say anything.... And you talk in other ways than just with words.

David: (looking startled) Well said, *habibu* (my friend). Come.


And thus began a pastoral relationship. The chaplain's relationship with David seems to have brought David closer to the hospital staff generally. In a few weeks David would be dead, with many of the staff, as well as the chaplain, keeping vigil over him in his last few days.

In David's last days he trusted the chaplain enough to share his difficult life story with her. He also allowed her to read parts of the

Torah to him. She says she did not push the 'religious' aspect of chaplaincy further. She felt that God was present and believed David felt it too, and that God had reentered his life. She wonders if she should have brought up the topic of God earlier and more intentionally to help David reach a more explicit reconciliation with his religion and God.

She felt that David projected the image of a strong and determined man, and that this was a defense against his loneliness, weakness, and the cancer that was killing him.

She notes that he did not take pain medication during and after their sessions, suggesting that her presence was therapeutic for him.

In her own discussion of the case, the chaplain says she considers "spirituality" as a kind of life force possessed by everyone, as in breath. She draws on derivations of the meaning of the word, stemming from the verb "to breathe."

## II. The Published Critiques

The co-editor critic (Steve Nolan) points out that this case is one of a patient's "total pain," drawing from Cicely Saunders, meaning physical as well as existential pain.

The chaplain critic (David Mitchell) applauds the chaplain's good use of silence, her "patience and presence creating a safe space." He wonders if the wider medical team was aware of the depth of the chaplain's work, implying of course that they needed to be.

The nurse critic (Barbara Pesut) writes that this case illustrates the quintessential outcome for palliative care, a peaceful, connected death. She also wonders if there was not more reciprocity in this pastoral relationship than is disclosed, that while the chaplain helped David connect with persons, David may have helped the chaplain see that God's connection is enduring and particularly strong within those who suffer.

# III. The Author's Perspective

I was moved by the chaplain's patience and tenacity. And I would guess that David found her a special gift at his life's end. One can hardly do better than that.

At the same time, there is a lot in the chaplain's thinking and doing that is equivalent to shooting oneself in the foot. For starters, I find it terribly jolting to read where the chaplain suggests in her introduction of herself that she has come to offer talk, listening, and prayer. Such an introduction seems designed to alienate most of the world's population, and even more of the more sensible among them. Isn't it quite enough to offer to visit, without specifying what should be implicit, namely talking and listening? And why add prayer? The invitation to prayer is destined to alienate most persons, especially persons in whom the chaplain is most likely interested.

Of course, there are those who are delighted to have someone pray with them. And there is certainly no warrant against their doing so. But such persons are not necessarily among the savviest or the most sensitive. Surely, if a particular person desires prayer, they can ask for it, and that surely can be negotiated. But there is no benefit in leading with the offer. To do so is to shoot oneself in the foot.

With the chaplain critic, I also applaud the chaplain's frequent use of silence as an instrument of communication.

As for the chaplain's wondering if she should have brought up the "topic of God" in David's last days and offered to help him reconcile to religion and God, praise be to all the gods that she did not. David, being who he was, might have blown off the relationship they had established had she made such a "religious" move. Everyone has a breaking point. This impulse on the chaplain's part is a matter she might consider looking into with a consultant.

And as for the chaplain's conclusion that at least God was *present* in David's last days, the presence or absence of God are metaphors that should not be taken at face value. The chaplain in this case is much too focused on the notion of the presence of God as something to be desired and sought after. It's a snare that is not helping her function well as a chaplain.

In seminary I once took a class under the famous Lutheran pastor, Paul Scherer, author of *Love is a Spendthrift*. He told a story one day about addressing a meeting of ministers, when at question time one young minister from the back of the room stood up and asked, "Dr. Scherer, how can we make God more present to members of our congregation?" Scherer said he responded, "Don't worry about God. He will take care of himself. The question is how *you* can become more present."

Theoretically, God must certainly be both present and absent in everything. The presence of God is a peculiar metaphor in that God is omnipresent, or omni-absent, each simultaneously. I recommend the chaplain read some of the more weighty and classic theologians like Paul Tillich and Karl Barth. They could help with her religious ideation. And I recommend she cease making facile judgments about the presence or absence of God anywhere. What really counted for David was the fact that the chaplain herself was *present*. And I venture to believe that she was a bearer of God's grace. But of that assertion I cannot be sure. What I am sure of is that she was indeed a bearer of grace, at the very least, *her* grace.

In spite of a certain amount of cloying piety, I believe the chaplain was an instrument of redemption for a broken man in his last days. I do believe she blessed his last days with care and grace. And it seems that she became the catalyst for the hospital itself to properly care for David in his last days. I am especially happy that she did not find a way to inflict prayer on David or on the hospital community at large. There was no need to gild the lily.

# CASE 9
# A Native American Family Attends to the Dying of Their Matriarch

## I. The Case

A Native American woman is dying, and the chaplain is called to minister to the family. Their presenting need seems to be for assistance in performing the death rituals of the family's particular tribe. The rituals are complex and time consuming. But the family is also Catholic. Thus, they also wait for the priest to arrive and perform the Catholic rituals. The Native American rite is supposed to be last, after the Catholic rite. But so is the Catholic rite. Neither ritual in this case is brief. During the long wait for the priest to arrive, the matriarch of the family asks the chaplain to pray, which he agrees to do. Though not clearly stated, it seems that the chaplain is now standing in for the Native American holy man, who also has been summoned.

The matriarch tells the chaplain to instruct the dying woman that it is ok to release her spirit. So the chaplain does as instructed, praying to the Great Spirit Mother-God, and finally signs off in the name of Christ. Eventually, a large number of family members drift in, along with a holy man and drummers. There is chanting and crying. The Catholic priest is already hours late and is delayed further by traffic. The family then decides to proceed with the Native American rites, with songs, chants, and ritual smudging. After some time the family requests another call to the priest, who is now reporting to be only 15 minutes from the hospital. The family asks the chaplain to lead in the Catholic Litany of the Saints while they wait. Near the end of the litany the priest finally arrives. He explained to the family what he would do, namely readings from scripture, renewal of baptismal vows, the Apostolic Blessing, intercessory prayers, the imposition of hands, the anointing with oil, the Lord's Prayer, and Prayer of

Commendation. In my own experience I have never known Catholic last rites to be so long and complicated.

The priest invited the Holy Man to stand next to him while he presided over the rituals. When the ritual was complete, the family directed that the life sustaining equipment be disconnected. These actions were accompanied by "blood-curdling shrieks" from the women present. The Holy Man then moved in to close the deceased's eyes, clip her hair, and change her covering. Instructions are given as to how the body should be treated in the morgue, and the chaplain assures them that their instructions will be honored.

The chaplain here functioned primarily as an administrator, first, in relation to the hospital staff, clarifying and enforcing the requests of the family, and second, in the triangular interface between the family and the Catholic and Native American rites and rituals. The administrative task is not to be despised, but it is certainly somewhat tangential to the primary task of the cure of souls.

Of particular interest is the history of the chaplain himself. He was previously a Catholic priest who left the Catholic Church and is currently in process of seeking to be received by the Episcopal Church.

## II. The Critics

The co-editor critic (Steve Nolan) assesses the chaplain as an invaluable resource to both the family and the institution. He characterizes the family as culturally Native American and religiously Catholic. I would think this assessment would be considered a slur against Native American religion. The critic characterized the chaplain as a willing student rather than a spiritual expert in the face of Native American spirituality, which seemed an apt characterization.

The chaplain critic (David Mitchell) thought that to persons outside the profession this case (and the previous two) would appear to be surprising and creative in-depth spiritual encounters. He contends that the chaplain in this case was skillful in balancing the Christian rites with Native American rites. This critic goes on to declare that spirituality is different from religion, and it may or may not include religion, and furthermore, our burden now is to understand the uniqueness of religion within the context of spiritual care. He goes on to add that spiritual pain is hard to define, yet we know it when we see it, specifically signs of anxiety, hopelessness, changes in character and demeanor, physical symptoms. He further adds that this case could be adapted as a tool for teaching on faith, belief, and culture at the end of life. Such cases, he says, "are a very valuable tool for 'earthing' theory in practice, and are particularly useful in the ethereal topic of spiritual care."

This critic seems confident that he knows the distinctions between spiritual and religious, though he keeps the secret to himself. I do concur with him on his final point, that spiritual is an ethereal material that requires "earthing." But I do not believe that he or anyone else has succeeded in accomplishing that task as yet. Furthermore, I do not believe anyone will be successful in earthing the ethereal. The effort itself is continuing to poison in the clinical pastoral movement.

The nurse critic (Barbara Pesut) calls the chaplain a spiritual broker, bridging the worlds of Catholic and Native American spirituality. It was all the more skillful, she says, in that the chaplain did not have the luxury of a long-term relationship. But she wishes the chaplain had reflected more of his grief over his loss of identity as a Catholic priest. The critic also wondered about a prevalence of positive emotions in this case (as in the previous two) and questioned how one might gauge the effectiveness of care that takes place *without* positive emotions such as might attend to a peaceful death.

## III.  The Author's Perspective

In this case the chaplain is relegated to the role of administrator, a useful role to be sure, but somewhat on the boundary of pastoral care and counseling, or as the authors prefer, "spiritual care."

The most noticeable dynamics in this case were rather covert, and certainly not identified. I refer to the struggle between the Native American tradition and the Catholic tradition. Though outwardly cordial, each representative of the respective traditions was seemingly determined to have the last word in the dying scene. It's an oft-repeated story, and it is actually a battle for preeminence. In the final scene, the Catholic priest invites the Native American holy man to stand beside him in a gesture of generosity. But, of course, the Catholic remained in charge. And when the Catholic priest completed his ritual, the Native American moved in to perform some final acts. It was a fascinating dance in the quest for preeminence. All in all, this seemed a clash of cultures: Catholic, Native American, modern medical. It did not seem like a happy fit. It had the marks of a border skirmish.

I remember the first funeral I ever conducted, as a very young man decades ago. It was a simple graveside service. When I pronounced the blessing over the open grave and thought I had written *fini* on the service, up strode a couple of Masons in ritual aprons and proceeded to do their hocus-pocus. I knew intuitively in that moment that the church and I were made mere preludes to the real thing. That would not have been possible in the church building, but at the grave it was open season.

The chaplain himself in this published case seemed happy to coordinate the time-consuming pair of rituals as well as provide hospitality to the numbers of family members, some of them expressing their grief in ways that would seem disturbing to other patients. He was also in the role of coordinator with hospital staff around the demands of the Native American death ritual.

The chaplain reports he did not function as a pastoral counselor or spiritual guide, but rather as a compassionate spiritual presence connecting with the family members on an affective level. Actually, he was a third string religious authority in this context, standing behind the Native American holy man and the Catholic priest. He demonstrated admirable restraint in maintaining his position as an ex-Catholic priest. Except for the "legality" of it, he could have done everything that the family waited so long for, the arrival of the "official" Catholic priest.

In conclusion, the chaplain writes that today he would probably not need to impose structured prayers on the family in the midst of their anxiety as they awaited the arrival of the priest. He says he would let them experience their anxiety. I think that a very insightful piece of self-supervision. However, the family did request these prayers while they awaited the officially authorized Catholic priest. It is not clear how he would have refused the request to lead in the litany while they awaited the Catholic priest.

The chaplain bore the burden of an all-day project that was basically administrative.

These Native Americans, powerless people in an alien culture, were able for once, perhaps, to assert their authority with audacity simply because the dominant culture is spooked by death and is not about to restrict their funeral rites. For once they got to do in a minor way what they succeeded in doing in a larger way to General Custer in the 19th century, but with impunity this time. In a small way, this was the revenge of the Indians.

# REFLECTIONS ON
# DAVID B. MCCURDY'S
## *Ethical Issues in Case Study Publication*

## I.

A final chapter of the book, entitled "Ethical Issues in Case Study Publication," by David B. McCurdy, argues that it is the chaplain's responsibility to write and publish case studies. Furthermore, he says that it is the chaplain's responsibility to share with the widest possible audience the emotional and spiritual impact of human encounters like those described in this book. Chaplains "have a duty to share this spirit or Spirit and these experiences," he says, and "whatever spirit or Spirit is at work in these relational spaces needs to be unveiled." We must show this work to an audience beyond that of the chaplaincy guild or even the medical world. Chaplains have a duty to share what they do. If I may place an editorial and cautionary parenthesis around his use of the category "spiritual," I can say that I believe the author is exactly correct on this matter.

## II.

But on another two points that the author makes, I dissent. He proposes, along with the co-editor, George Fitchett, that pastoral care professionals who publish clinical cases should seek prior approval from the Institutional Review Boards (IRB) of the institutions where they work. Yet history documents that when such permissions to publish pastoral care and counseling cases has been requested of an IRB, it has refused to act, declaring that such cases are not research, and permission unnecessary. Nevertheless, the writer continues to say, astonishingly, "It remains wise for chaplains to consult their local IRBs or an equivalent body regarding plans for publication." I am puzzled by this apparent need for third-party approbation to share clinical pastoral cases. It suggests to me a failure of professional authority. Why would anyone beg for permission to publish from an institution that has declared that the freedom to publish already exists? This suggests to me a hidden agenda. Does this mean that chaplains, low on the medical establishment's pecking order, are now begging for more professional status and recognition that IRB approval might provide them? Religious authorities and leaders must realize that they are forever on the fringe of the scientific arena and will always be under a certain amount of suspicion simply because they represent a field and a tradition that is mostly beyond the reach of hard science. Psychiatry is held in similar suspicion, if less so.

In spite of all this, McCurdy and Fitchett continue doggedly to insist that chaplains petition IRBs for permission to publish case studies.

## III.

The passion of McCurdy and Fitchett, evidenced as well from earlier writing, is to insert chaplains into the prestigious arena of scientific medicine and its quality control. This wish is misguided, and betrays a shallow view of pastoral care and counseling. In medical research, as surveilled by IRBs, the unconscious of the physician is not a part of what is examined, measured, or evaluated. However, any third-party assessment of pastoral care and counseling inevitably will scrutinize the person of the pastor, including data suggestive of unconscious processes impinging for good or for ill on the patient or client relationship.

McCurdy and Fitchett, it seems, view pastoral care and counseling as an external process, a kind of distribution of religious goods, such as prayer and sacraments, along with generalized comforting conversation or presence. Such a posture in the context of patient work is alien to the Boisen tradition of clinical pastoral training. In that tradition, the pastor cannot be prepared entirely by didactic instruction. The person of the pastor herself is the primary tool in pastoral care and counseling, and by the same token, the person of the pastor is the principal focus of training. This is the genius of the Boisonite clinical pastoral training movement. This is something that McCurdy and Fitchett appear not to grasp.

Consequently, this kind of patient work is not material that an IRB would know what to do with. It is the kind of work that is radically different from cardiovascular surgery, where new procedures might be experimented with under surveillance of an IRB and where the person of the physician, and his or her neuroses, is of little interest or concern. No IRB would know how to assess the process that takes place when a chaplain engages a patient therapeutically and, therefore, where the soul or psyche or person of a pastoral clinician engages a patient.

# IV.

A second recommendation McCurdy makes, supported by Fitchett, is for authors of clinical cases to enlist permission to publish from patients who are the subjects of such case write-ups. The author recommends that permissions be sought late in the pastoral relationship, after a bond has been established. It is possible to get such permissions in an ongoing relationship, he argues, and even to make the request itself "a part of the spiritual care." And astonishingly, the author adds that either written or verbal permission would suffice. (My view is that a patient's verbal permission for the chaplain to disclose to the public the patient's personal medical data, even anonymously, would be utterly worthless.)

Further complicating any such request of a patient for permission to publish is the fact that there are almost always third parties involved—relatives and friends—who are typically but not directly participating in a one-to-one pastoral relationship, but who might be affected adversely by public disclosure of the case.

As an example, in Case 7, Lee's brother, Ed, participated in the activities around the death of their father, but was emotionally unavailable and inscrutably distant. Ed likely would have strong objections to his being publicly portrayed as an unfeeling son, sleepwalking through his father's funeral, accompanied by a daughter adored by her father. The fact is, if patients or clients were to be informed of the use of their story in publication, it is not only the patient who would need to sign a release but also everyone mentioned or even indirectly alluded to in the case.

This proposal to request patient permission to publish is even worse than the lust for IRB approval. It is bound to be disruptive to the pastoral and therapeutic relationship. And it is bound to stir up concerns in the patient that would add to whatever travails the patient is experiencing already.

It is also noteworthy that only two of the nine cases in the book indicate that the chaplain sought patient approval for the publishing of their case. In Case 1, that of 12-year-old LeeAnn, the patient was even given permission, after reading the case, to veto the publication if she wished. I suspect that the courts would consider a 12-year-old incapable of granting permission for anything to be published that might affect her life negatively in the future. Furthermore, what patient is strong enough or wise enough to contemplate examining the unconscious of his or her minister, counselor, or therapist? And how could a 12-year-old, or any patient for that matter, deliberate on the possible errors in the treatment course?

For a chaplain purposely to bring a patient into a discussion of his or her own idiosyncrasies and failures as a counselor would mean the likely end of the pastoral relationship. How could a patient or client sit in on a discussion of the shortcomings of his or her counselor? Such an exposure and evaluation of the pastoral counseling treatment would contaminate the counseling relationship and confuse roles. The patient would become the quasi-supervisor and evaluator, and the chaplain would become the counselee. This is a serious error. An attempt to take this route would open a can of worms that would bring nothing good.

The author's most candid statement, in conclusion, is that there is more to be learned about what it means to respect all case participants in publishing case studies. He got that right.

# V.

This essay is confused and confusing at a number of points.

First, its author is listed as McCurdy, but at points in the essay "we" is used for authorship, referring to both Fitchett and McCurdy. Overall, the essay is an amalgam of both author's views. If there are any differences between the two, they were not evident. It seems that the declaration of authorship at the beginning should have named both authors.

Second, as already stated above, the authors continue to advocate seeking IRB approval for publication of pastoral cases, in spite of the failure to achieve such approval, and indeed the judgment by IRBs that such approval is not called for.

Third, the authors advocate seeking patient approval for the publishing of cases, even as they acknowledge that some patients are in no condition to give such approval, and others are not actually competent to grant such approval.

Fourth, as if to contradict everything else they write about sharing their pastoral work with IRBs and patients alike, they propose that the counseling relationship be kept inviolably private. They appeal to the Christian medieval tradition of the absolute privacy of the confessional, suggesting that Christian patients at least should have the benefit of such level of confidentiality. Though the authors do not say so, the advantage to this stance would be that no one would be in a position to criticize.

Fifth, the authors show no awareness whatsoever of the boundary problems that emerge when pastoral counseling cases are shared with patient or client—namely, the part of the case where the counselor reflects on his or her own history and unconscious processes as they relate to the case at hand. No patient or counselee should be privy to the emotional and psychological idiosyncrasies of his or her counselor.

At the beginning of this chapter the authors proclaimed the importance of sharing clinical data among professionals. By the end of the paper they seek to be governed by Institutional Review Boards and the patients themselves. If such a state of affairs came to pass, there would be no further clinical pastoral training as we have known it.

Should the clinical pastoral movement elect to follow the guidance of McCurdy and Fitchett, it will in effect sign its own death warrant. No longer will the richest of cases be available for discussion, and no longer will the character and make-up of the pastoral clinician be part of the clinical investigation. Pastoral clinicians will then be reduced to the role of peddlers of religious artifacts and platitudes. And of course, prayers. The success of McCurdy and Fitchett will represent the end, after a century, of the Boisonite movement.

# GENERAL CRITICISM OF THE BOOK
## *Spiritual Care in Practice:*
## *Case Studies in Healthcare Chaplaincy*

## I.

The first general criticism that must be made of this volume is that none of its nine cases is situated in a non-Christian context. And each of the chaplains is identifiably Christian. One case is situated in a family espousing a mix of Roman Catholic and Native American religion, and one case portrays a Jewish patient who has by his own account given up all religion. But that is the extent of any kind of pastoral work beyond the bounds of Christianity. In that regard, the collection is hardly representative of what the typical chaplain faces in the day-to-day work as a chaplain in the United States. It certainly does not represent the tough challenges that the typical chaplain faces because of the multiple manifestations of religion currently emerging in this country.

## II.

The second criticism that must be made is that the 27 published critiques of the 9 cases are on balance extraordinarily weak. Except for the work of one of the seven critics, the criticisms were generally effete and overly laudatory. It's as if the presenting chaplains needed to be coddled, or even encouraged, lest they lose heart. Thus, the work as a whole hardly represents the best of the American clinical pastoral training movement spawned by Anton Boisen. The clinical training of the Boisen movement changed the lives of developing pastors and religious leaders. Historically, the clinician-in-training who presented a case for supervision or consultation typically found not only the work itself critiqued but also the clinician's own personal identity placed under scrutiny. Clinical training was powerfully engaging personally, and hardly anyone left a well-conducted training experience without being changed. By contrast, very few of the published critiques in the book, *Spiritual Care in Practice,* will have any significant effect on the presenting chaplain personally. The self of the chaplain was not engaged. Nor was the clinical work itself subjected to serious criticism. This failure to embody the rich tradition of strong criticism that was the singular mark of the Boisen tradition of clinical pastoral training actually is astonishing and inexplicable, given that the editors themselves were allegedly products of that movement.

I recall my own early days as a seminarian. After their first year of study, several of my close friends in seminary went off for a summer of clinical training at the Medical College of Virginia. I was scheduled to go as well, but I informed the seminary dean that I was serving two small churches in rural Virginia and suggested to him that I was engaged in my own clinical experience. The dean, clearly uninformed about the value of clinical training, was persuaded and gave me a bye on the summer of training. In September, when I reunited with my friends, I was caught off guard, almost stunned. My friends were different. It was nothing I could put my finger on. They were not unfriendly to me at all. Yet they seemed to see the world a bit differently than before. I sensed in that moment that I had missed something important and would eventually have to undergo clinical training myself. I finally did, seven years and many blunders later.

The chaplains whose cases appear in this collection do not have the subtle marks of persons who have undergone clinical training. Of course the reality is that there is training and *there is training.* In the era when I was a seminarian, most (but not all) clinical training programs were quite rigorous. That is no longer the case. One easily can find a training program that might properly be labeled "clinical training light." Such programs may well be in the majority at present.

I suspect, however, that an additional reason the published critiques as a whole were so weak was the reluctance to risk the possible damage to the reputations of nine working chaplains who presented their work. In my view, it would have been far more felicitous to make the chaplains anonymous, just as the patients were. In that way, any potential insult to their reputations would be avoided. Privacy and confidentiality are requisites in any training program. It is difficult enough to absorb serious criticism within the confines of a small clinical group. Being criticized seriously before the whole world is intolerable for many.

# III.

This work is chock full of references and footnotes that are utterly useless. One would have to presume that someone among the editorial staff instructed the authors to pad the writing with footnotes and citations in order for their product to appear credible to the world of scholarship. If so, the instruction backfired. The use of so many banal citations actually makes the various authors appear either uninformed or sycophantish. For example, why would anyone need a footnote in a published work to reinforce the following claims?

"In responding to patient needs, one must allow time and engage in attentive listening," citing Mundle and Smith (2013).

"It is not unusual for strong emotions to emerge in this kind of situation [when patients believe that hospital staff are acting against their wishes]," citing Coughlan and Ali (2009).

Authorities found that, "in terms of family perspectives on dying, spiritual support was important to families," citing Wilson and Daley (1999).

I found these and similar banal citations annoying, useless, and reflecting poorly on the author's judgment. I fully expected to find some authority cited, giving approval for the publication of books on pastoral care and counseling.

# IV.

Of the nine cases presented, only one case engages issues of sexual behavior, and in that case it is homosexual behavior. One other case references homosexuality as a background matter that does not directly shape the course of pastoral care. The complete absence of any issues related to heterosexual behavior of any sort in any of the cases is stunning. The silence is deafening.

Most of the pastoral counselors and chaplains I talk with tell me that most of their counseling work involves issues attending to heterosexual behavior.

This stark discrepancy between what is apparently happening in the real world and what is represented in these nine cases is, I believe, a poignant commentary on our times, as well as a commentary on this book. I believe there is an explanation for this lacuna.

After the flowering of the sexual revolution in the '70s and '80s, the feminist movement then gained ascendancy in the clinical pastoral training movement, which it currently holds, and in alliance with male homosexuals has largely inhibited serious and judicious discussion of male heterosexual behavior. The inhibition has resulted in a muffling of thoughtful discussion of the proper boundaries of heterosexual males in general. Thus, serious and considered discussion of the ethics of heterosexual male behavior has gone into eclipse. The eclipse has resulted in critical ethical decision-making being done in the closet, out of public view. The consequences have been a number of grievous injustices levied against heterosexual males.

The irony here is that the founder of clinical pastoral training, Anton Boisen, became what he was because of continuing struggles with his own sexuality, in this case his heterosexuality. Furthermore, sexual issues were preeminent and prolific in the first half century of the clinical training movement. I have argued elsewhere* that Boisen's sexual struggles, transparent as they were, prepared American Protestantism for the sexual revolution to come. The mainstream Protestant churches were ready and prepared for the '60s in ways that other religions, and the secular social order, were not.

By the '90s, however, some of the more aggressive feminists, allied with elements of the homosexual community, had gained the dominance in the clinical pastoral world, and recklessly began targeting males as sexual predators. The result was that heterosexual males generally became largely mute and went underground with regard to their sexual behavior. I believe that this silence largely continues and is reflected in the choice of this collection of nine cases in the Fitchett-Nolan book.

*Sexual Liberation: The Scandal of Christendom, Praeger Press, 2007

# EPILOGUE: THE SPIRITUAL PROBLEM

## I.

If this book being critiqued, *Spiritual Care in Practice,* had been written a generation ago, it almost certainly would have carried the title *Pastoral Care and Counseling in Practice.* But the cultural landscape has shifted in a generation, and the word "pastoral" has been eclipsed by "spiritual." The pressure for this change came at the turn of the century, fifteen years ago. A number of those in leadership in the pastoral care and counseling community were concerned that "pastoral" was too much rooted in Christianity, and that "spiritual" was a more universal category. Consequently, they requested the Joint Commission on the Accreditation of Healthcare Organizations (JCAHO) to change its public terminology in describing chaplaincy roles from "pastoral care and counseling" to "spiritual care." The JCAHO complied. Many, but not all, chaplain departments in hospitals across the land changed names of their chaplaincy departments from "Department of Pastoral Care and Counseling" to "Department of Spiritual Care." The contention that "pastoral" was too restrictively Christian and that "spiritual" embraced all religions was an arguable point, but very ill conceived.

Words are strange artifacts. They change through time, for good and for ill. Some words are quite concrete and specific; others are malleable and have multiple connotations. "Spiritual" and "spirituality" lend themselves to multiple connotations, depending on context. It's a very fluid and troublesome category. For that reason, it often is difficult to know what the speaker or writer wants to say when the word "spiritual" or "spirituality" is spoken or written.

"Pastoral" for example, is not so fluid a word. Its principal connotation is shepherding, husbandry, caring for the sheep and other animals, as well as caring for crops. The central motif is the shepherd caring for the flock. Both Judaism and Christianity picked up this motif and used it for the model of religious leadership. Biblical literature is replete with references to shepherd and sheep. Religious leaders are compared with shepherds. Jesus became the good shepherd. This metaphor is not alien to Muslims, who also venerate the Bible. Buddhists and Hindus would have no theological basis for disdaining such a symbol. They, too, support teachers and guides who care for the flocks of their followers. It is a very natural and humane metaphor, neither aggressive nor predatory, nor intrinsically linked to Christianity. Beethoven's Pastoral Symphony is in no way linked to Christianity. Furthermore, the metaphor is one with its feet very much on the ground, so to speak.

Enter "spiritual." The word itself is in bad odor; the reason being that it has through history and usage migrated from this earthly home to some never-never land, the arena of the spirits. A "spiritualist" is one who communes with those dwelling in that never-never-land of ghosts and specters. That's a very troubling connotation for the word, especially for those who prefer not to dwell with ghosts. The fact is that one cannot use the word spiritual without causing, at very least, a slight echo of this spiritualism.

I contend, therefore, that the several chaplains whose clinical cases appear in this collection were all to one degree or another tainted by connotations of ghostliness, and the world of spirits. The consequence of that taint is that the patient will lean toward conceiving of the chaplain as an emissary of some other—ghostly—world. I believe such connotations radically undermine the authentic work of pastoral care and counseling. Who would want a shepherd who is not focused on this world? Such a shepherd is apt to have the animals in his care carried off by wild animals.

"Spiritual" was not always so disembodied, so emasculated, so devoid of vigor, so devoid of earthiness. But words change through history. The word's etymology is strong. Its stellar ancestry extends back to the Hebrew *ruah,* alluding to life-giving breath given to mankind by God. Breathing thus defines spiritual in the biblical texts. So also in Greek; the word spirit is *pneuma,* alluding to breath and lungs. Those who are filled with spirit breathe deeply. As centuries passed the word began losing its earthly footing and began to migrate to other realms, to supernatural arenas. Thus, spirit in German became *geist,* and from German it became ghost in English, and thus the Holy

Ghost. From that point, the connotation of spirit as the enlivening force of life, or breath, was mostly lost. The word and its power migrated to the arena of the disembodied. It was a long journey from spirit as the breath of life breathed into human lungs in the moment of creation to spirit as ghostly specters dwelling in the world of the disembodied. This etymological decompensation of the word "spiritual" undermines all pastoral care and counseling that employ the label "spiritual."

It is noteworthy that in Case 8, the chaplain describes David's "spirituality" quite aptly as a life force. The chaplain's problem is that she simply cannot assign to a word her preferred connotations. Each hearer will assign connotations to a word, one that is determined by common usage. Unfortunately for us all, spirituality generally does not connote life force. It connotes, for the most part, some ghostly world.

Norman O. Brown famously wrote, "Goodbye Holy Ghost. *Veni creator spiritus,*" as he tried to disassociate himself from ghosts and recover the earlier vital connotations of *spiritus.*

Paul Tillich wrote that the only modern usage of the word "spirit" that captures its ancient power is the reference to a horse that is "spirited." A horse that is spirited is full of himself, full of horse-ness. That horse is not a ghost horse, nor cavorting with ghosts. Thus, Tillich advised against using the word "spiritual" in attempts to communicate.

We must not, of course, become too anal or rigid about "spiritual" or any other word. Most words have some fluidity, a kind of music that attends to them, with major and minor connotations and associations. We should not fall into literalism. On occasion "spiritual" does carry authentic overtones. Much depends on context. Nevertheless, "spiritual" and "spirituality" are *mostly if not entirely* washed up as words of power in current usage. We wish it weren't so, but wishing accomplishes nothing.

Thus, the change from "Pastoral Care and Counseling" to "Spiritual Care" represents a net loss to the entire field of religious leadership and clinical pastoral training.

# II.

Much of a word's meaning depends on context. How a word is situated in context or in the conversation determines to some extent its meaning and power.

However, the slogan "spiritual but not religious" is a trickster's word game. It's a denigration of religion by replacing it with something without clear definition that looks awfully like, well yes, *religion.* Anyone committed to integrity in communication should push back on any claim of "spiritual but not religious" as an attempt at fraudulent communication.

For persons to claim that they are not religious is perfectly reasonable. Such a claim communicates clearly a disassociation from any religious group or religious ideology. But those who claim not to be religious but insist they are spiritual are engaging in garbled communication, and obfuscation. The innuendo is that such persons have found something better than religion, or something that replaces religion. But what is that something? Religious obfuscation. The category "spiritual" has no *there* there. It can mean almost anything, or almost nothing. We use words to communicate. When words lose the power to communicate, we are no longer communicating.

In a personal conversation with some particular folks who claimed to be "spiritual but not religious," they reported to me their belief that their dead loved ones, in this instance one who had recently died, was waiting for them in heaven and was daily watching over them. They claimed, in a presumably rational conversation, to believe that the recently deceased was making a place for them in heaven when it also came time for them to die. How that qualifies as "spiritual but not religious" baffles rational thought. What they communicated was that they were religious while declaring that they were not religious. I have a suspicion that "spiritual but not religious" might mean that the speaker has invented his own idiosyncratic religion to suit himself, the rest of the world be damned. If that's the case, one should say so, rather than resort to obfuscation.

A declaration of "not religious" is a clear communication. Persons who declare to be not religious may have some kind of value system or a set of benchmarks to buttress their integrity. They may have one of a number of mandates that guides their lives, with reference to God or religion not being one of them. That's certainly an acceptable stance for any person to take, and a stance that communicates clearly and with integrity.

The argument is made by some of the authors of *Spiritual Care in Practice* that spirituality is not the same thing as religion. That is a fair enough point of departure. So, if spirituality is not a form of religion, what exactly is it? In common usage today I do not believe that the concept of spirituality has a discernible definition. It is defined as an oblong blur. Or it is defined by whoever chooses to define it, with all definitions accepted as fair game. Now that seems to me to be a form of semantic schizophrenia, the allowance for a particular word to mean whatever the speaker wants it to mean. This is a narcissist's dream: a major word in common usage meaning whatever in the world the speaker wants it to mean.

Then there is the spirituality-not-religion movement in general. The suggestion here is that religion is a malevolent force in the world whereas spirituality is benign. We should remember that Nazism was a very spiritual movement with frequent references to God as well. Hitler's army had *"Gott Mit Uns"* (*"God with Us"*) emblazoned on its tanks, and his soldiers the same on their belt buckles.

Language is a communal activity. It is very difficult, or impossible, for one person or few persons to force meaning into words, or to revive old words, or to create new ones. Like the tides, language seems to have a life of its own. So it is likely that we are all cursed with the albatross of spirituality, at least for now, until it dawns on enough thinking people that the word has no more value than Confederate money. In the meantime, we will just have to wait and endure. In the meantime, however, we can be sure that people who pontificate about spirituality are mostly talking to themselves, and we need not take them seriously.

# III.

So why did I give to this book the subtitle *"The Soul of Pastoral Care and Counseling"*? Could I just as well have written the "spirit" of pastoral care and counseling? Each category, spirit and soul, is of course quite ephemeral. Neither is an object that can be examined. Each has connotations that take the mind somewhere else. There is, of course, no objective soul as far as anyone knows, and neither is there any objective spirit. Yet each in its own idiosyncratic way speaks to a need in the human psyche. Soul is closer to the earth in current usage, as in "soul food," the food that expresses the affirmation of African American culture, oppressed as it has been, but remaining affirmative. Spirit, as already belabored upon, is too close to the ghostly realm to be weighty for rational persons. Of the two religious categories, soul and spirit, each one problematic, soul is the richer one, and less problematic.

# IV.

The chaplain critic, David Mitchell, writes in favor of case studies, because case studies, he says, are a valuable tool for "earthing" theory in practice, and as he puts it, "particularly the ethereal topic of spiritual care." I believe that Mitchell performed us all a service in making this observation. Spirituality is indeed ethereal, out of this world, in the ether. And since most of those who pontificate on spirituality are untrained in space science, we then can be sure that they know little or nothing of what they speak. "Earthing" is indeed what spirituality begs for. But the more we use the word the farther from the earth it drifts.

# V.

We know what pastoral persons do. They care for a flock, some kind of flock, attending to its general welfare, watching particularly over the young, the weak, and the sick among them. Pastoral is a very rich word, both today and far back in history.

We have no idea what spiritual persons do. We suspect they reflect on the unseen world up there, out there. But we don't know what they see, if anything. And we don't really know what they care about, or what they are committed to. Spiritual is a category of obfuscation.

Pastoral persons are focused and alert, like Kierkegaard's proverbial dog, for what the master next commands them to do. Spiritual persons, on the other hand, are focused on what favors they might get from the gods. The world is in desperate need for more *pastoral* persons, to care for and shepherd the distressed, the sick, the broken, and the lost. As for *spiritual* persons, we have enough already.

# ABOUT THE AUTHOR

**Raymond J. Lawrence** is a clinical pastoral supervisor and pastoral psychotherapist, former Director of Pastoral Care at New York Presbyterian Hospital, founder of the College of Pastoral Supervision and Psychotherapy, author of *The Poisoning of Eros: Sexual Values in Conflict,* and *Sexual Liberation: the Scandal of Christendom.* He is also the author of various journal and book essays, as well as a number of opinion pieces in various newspapers. He has been an Episcopal clergyman for over half a century. You can begin a conversation with him at lawrence@cpsp.org.

Made in the USA
Middletown, DE
06 August 2024

58610659R00051